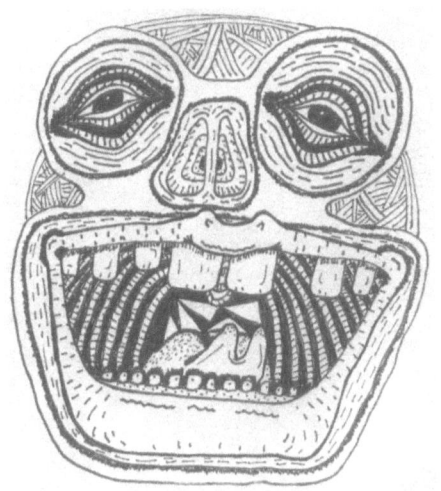

My name is Vaughn, and this is my art.

I've been sketching for about 3 years now, and my work has been constantly evolving.

I start with an idea and constantly change it.

I also start by drawing something random and build off of it.

I like human forms, patterns and shapes.

Detail is key.

What do you think?

Let's go back in time.

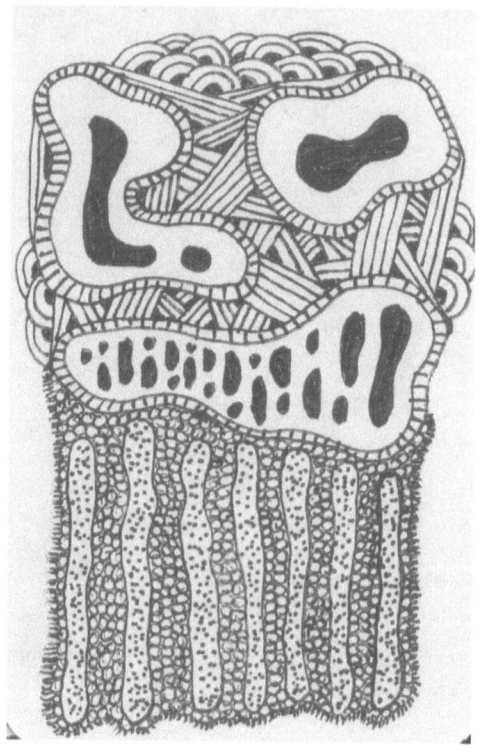

e work you will see is in no chronological order, but they start with ꜀ most recent drawings and go backwards to some of my earlier drawings.

In these first few sketches, I have been fixated on patterns, specifically lines.

usually incorporate figures and/or forms in my drawings, so I used patterns to create the overall shape and form, or I would simply fill the space with lines.

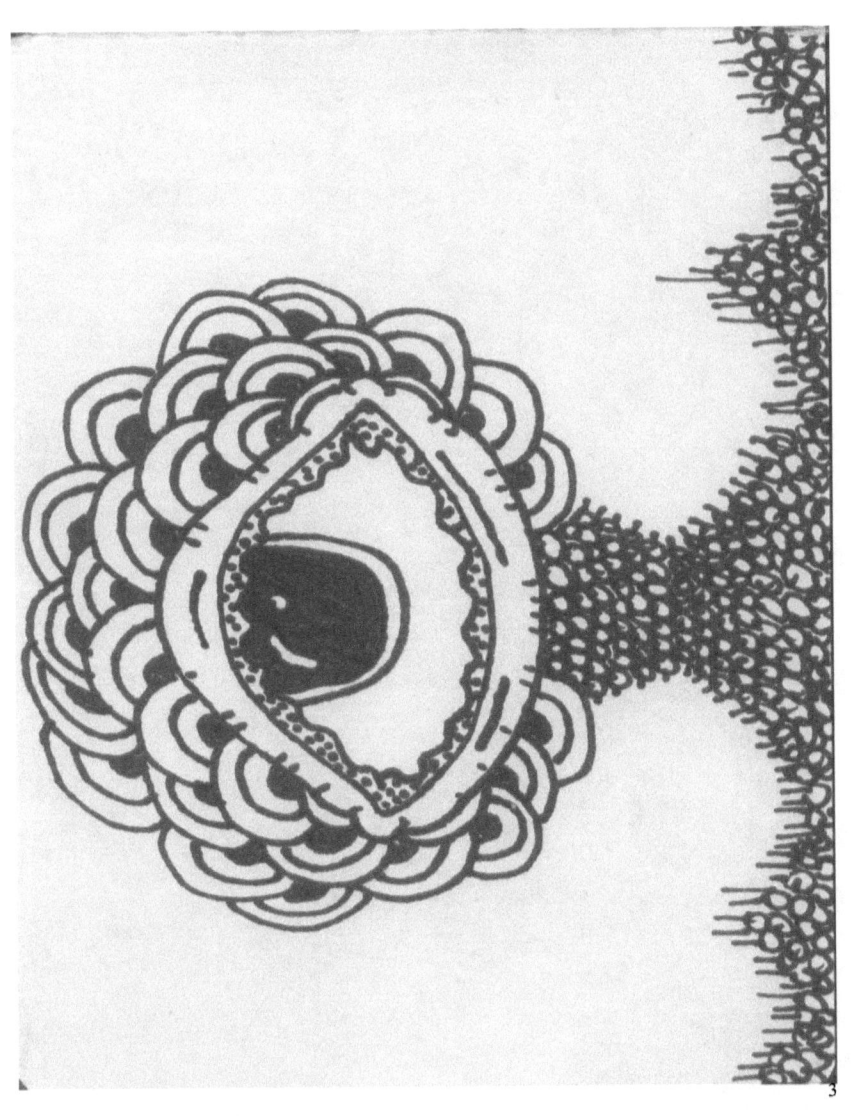

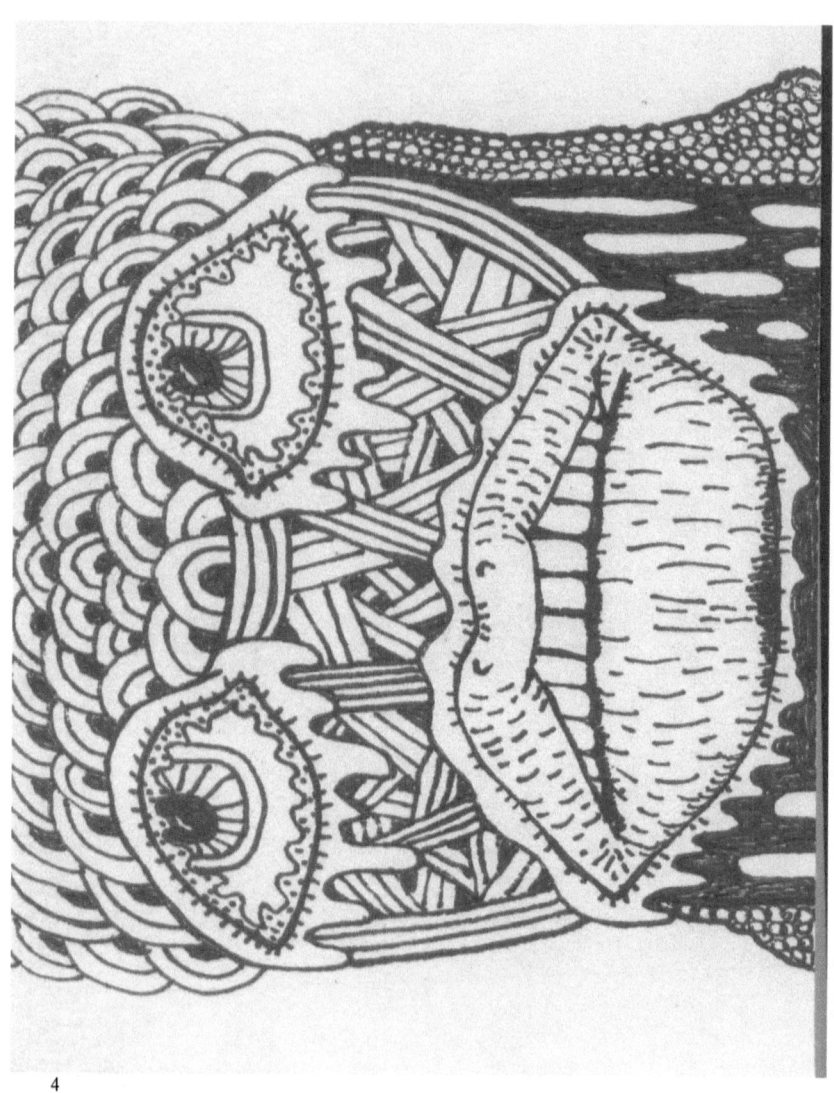

4

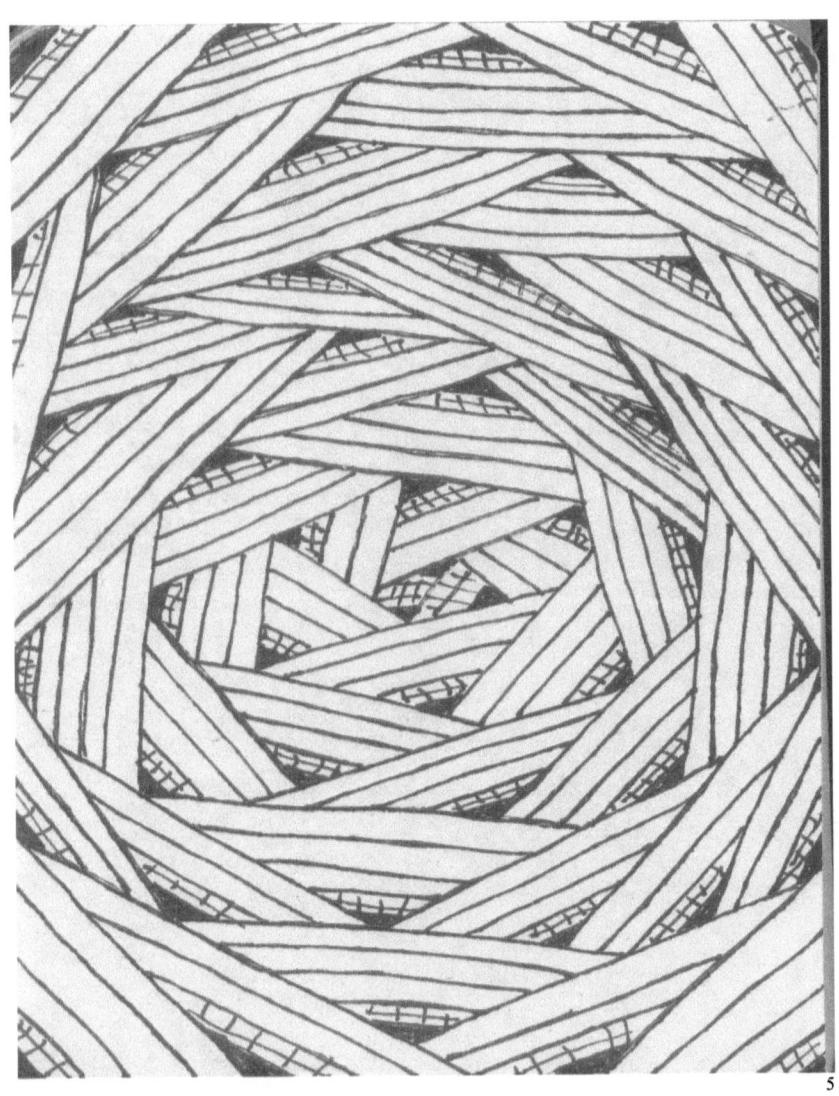

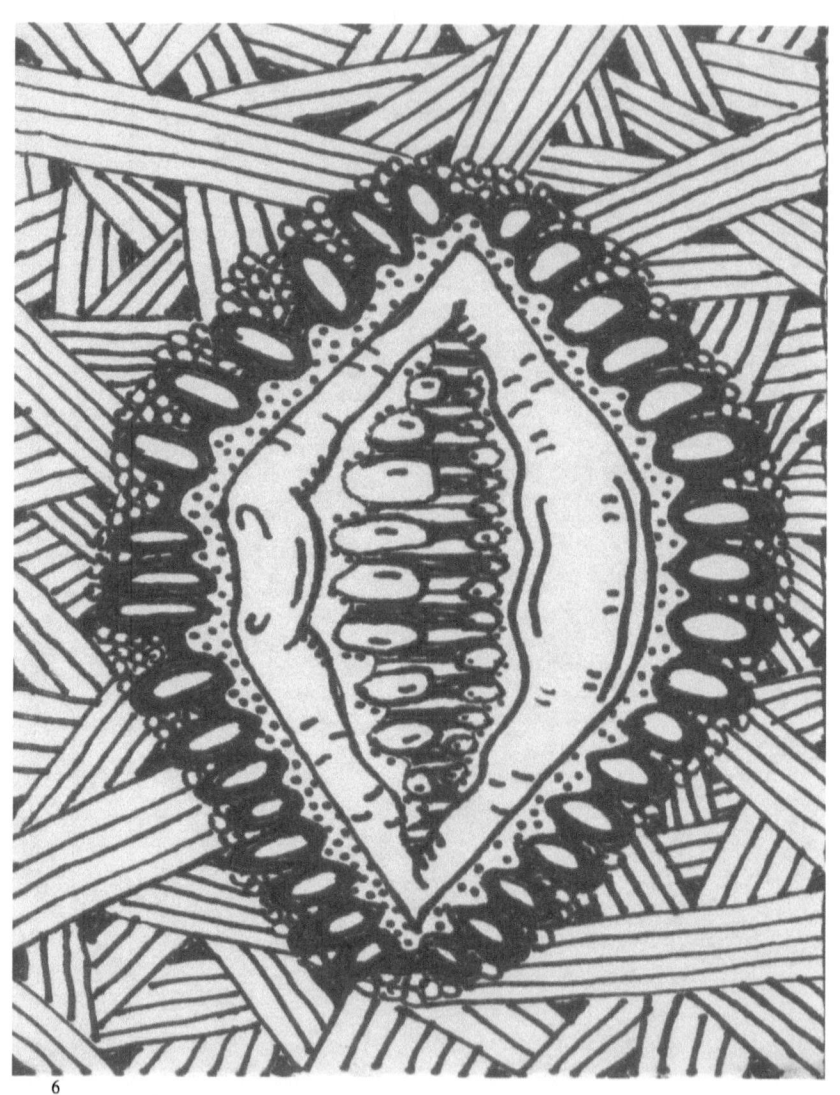

6

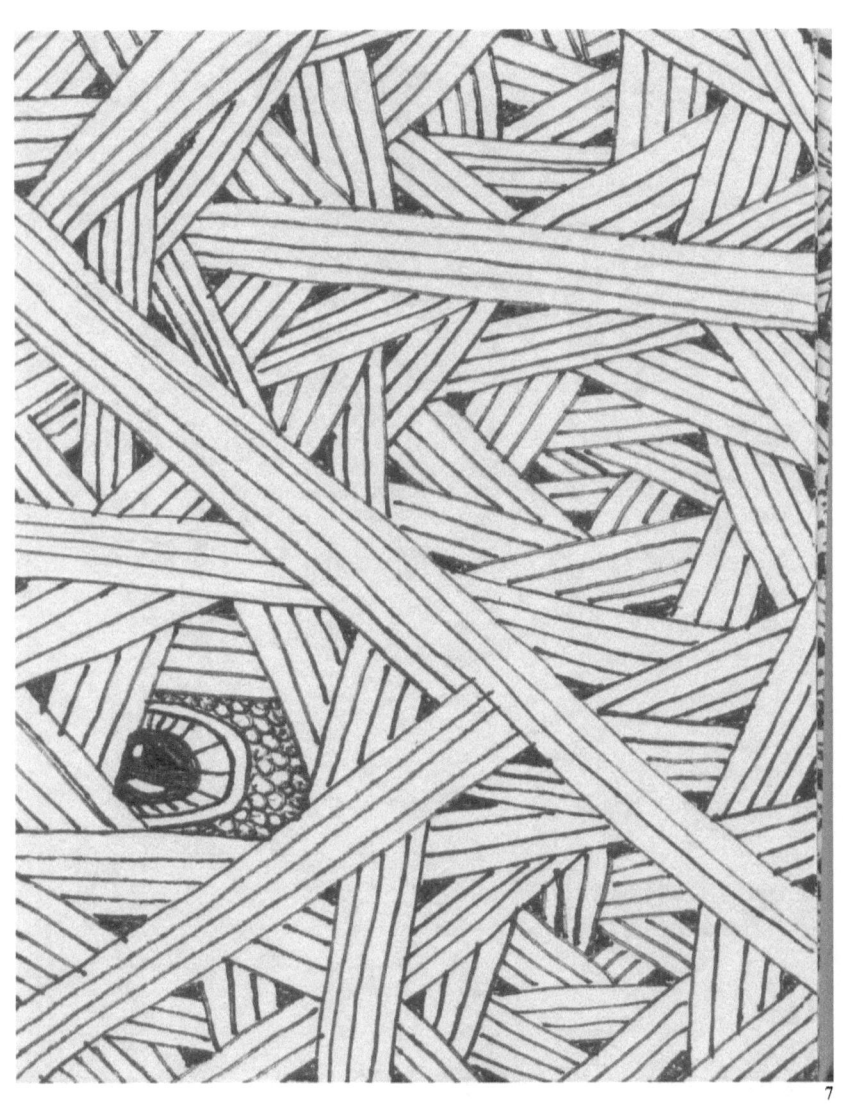

7

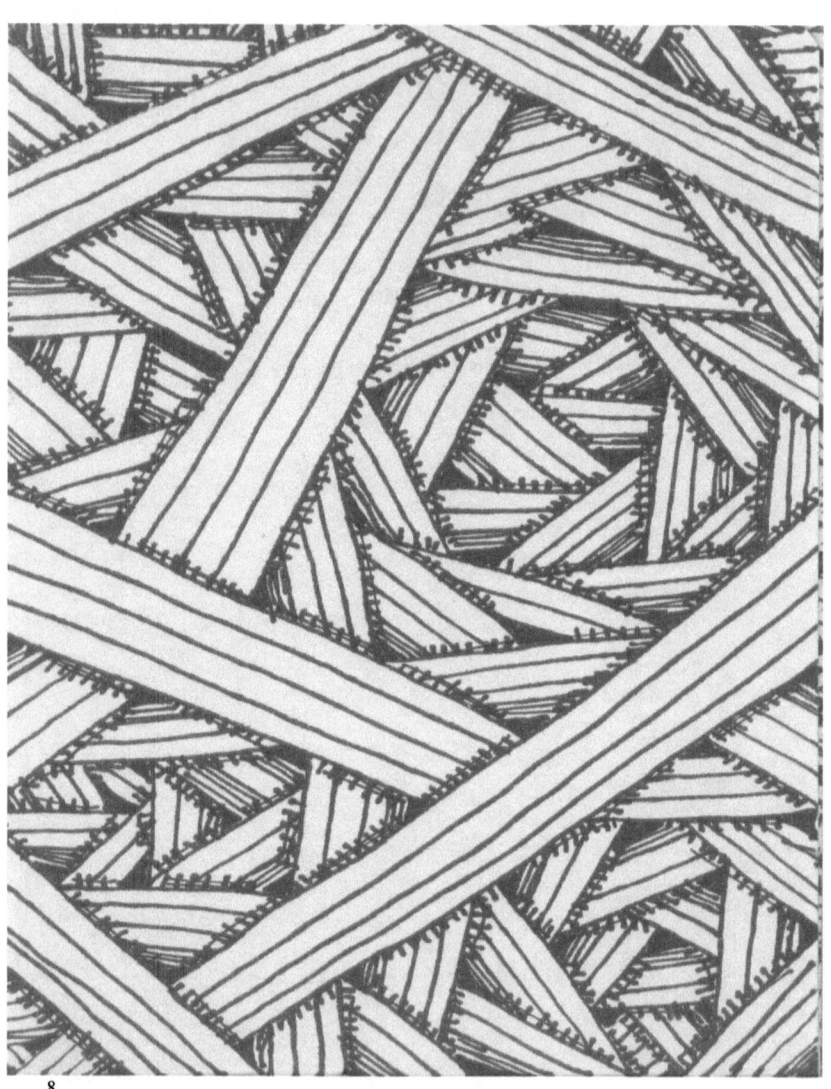

8

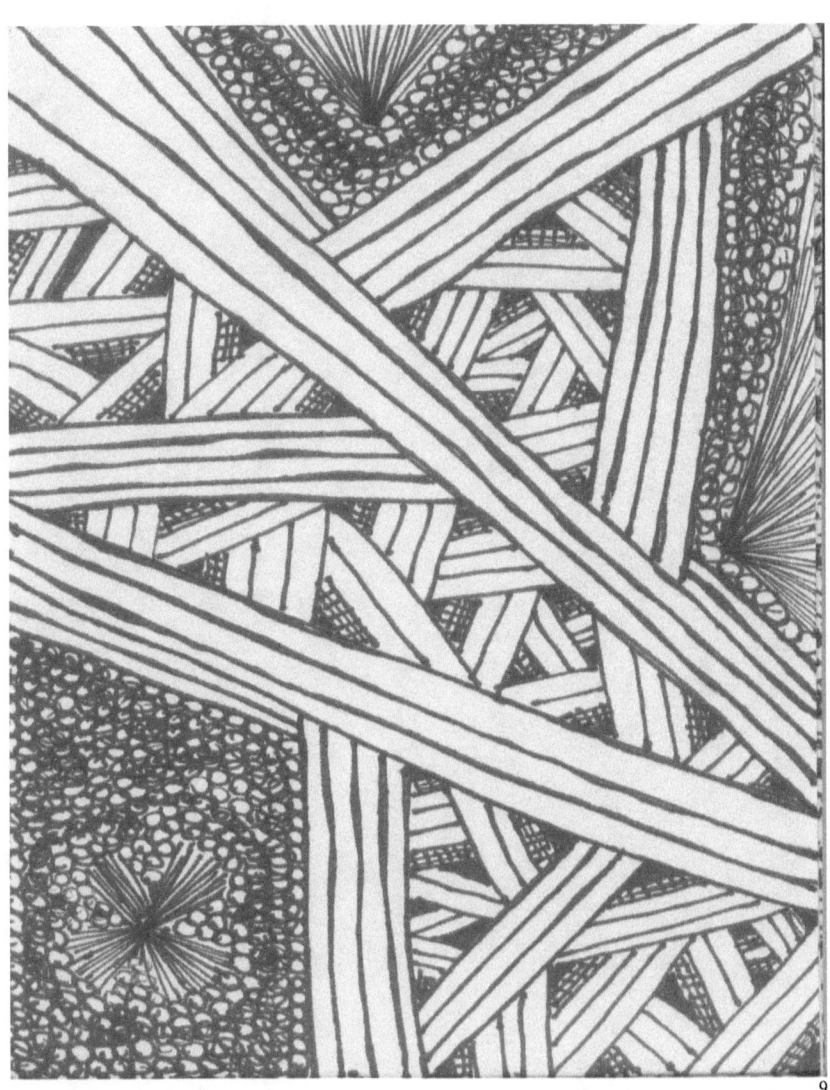

9

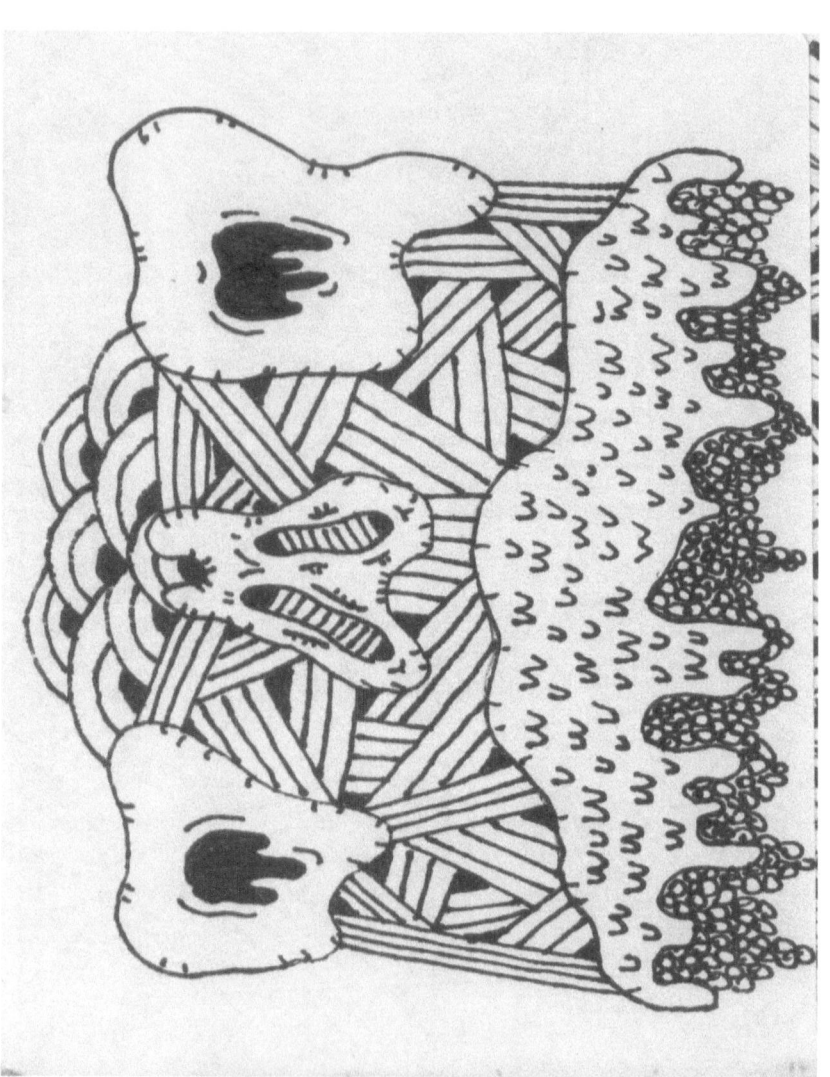

10

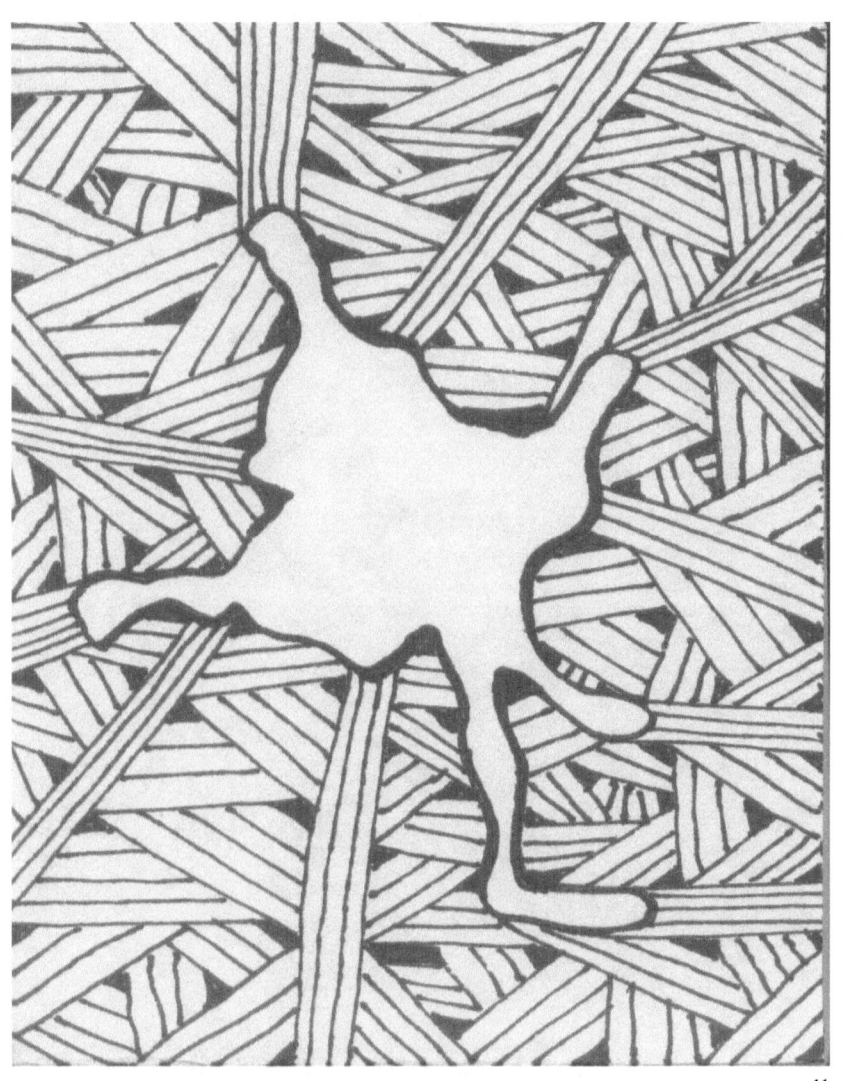

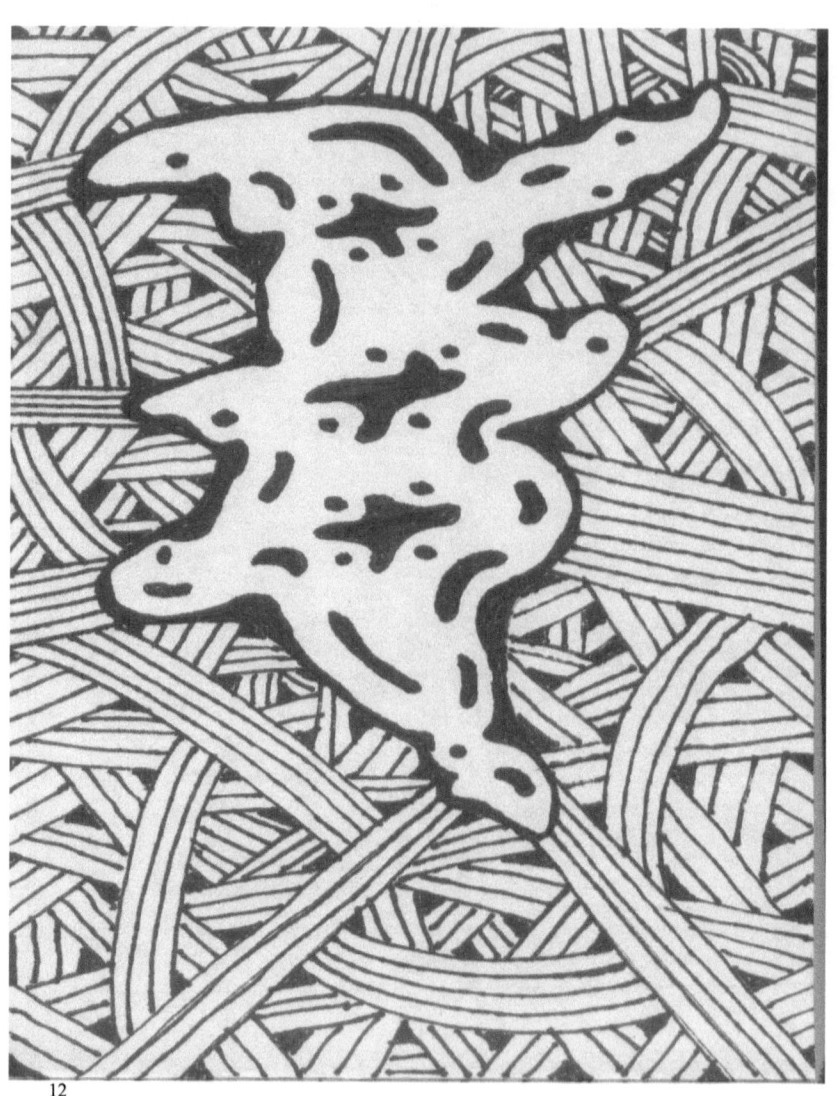

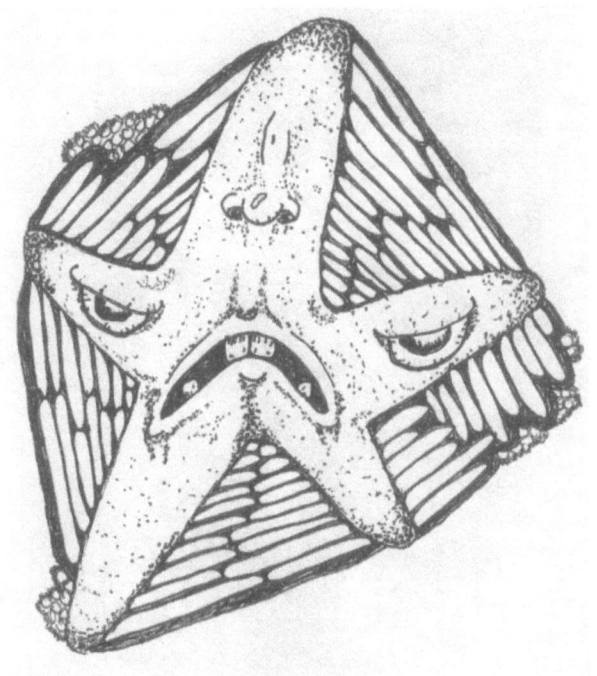

What started my growing interest in patterns is the next set of drawings. You can see how my images progressed in the manner that they have.

The majority of my artwork is highly influenced by the styles of other artists I know or see online. I find out the designs, patterns, and executions of their ideas and ultimately assimilate the ones I like into my own artwork.

My art has no real meaning; it is merely the flow of my imagination.

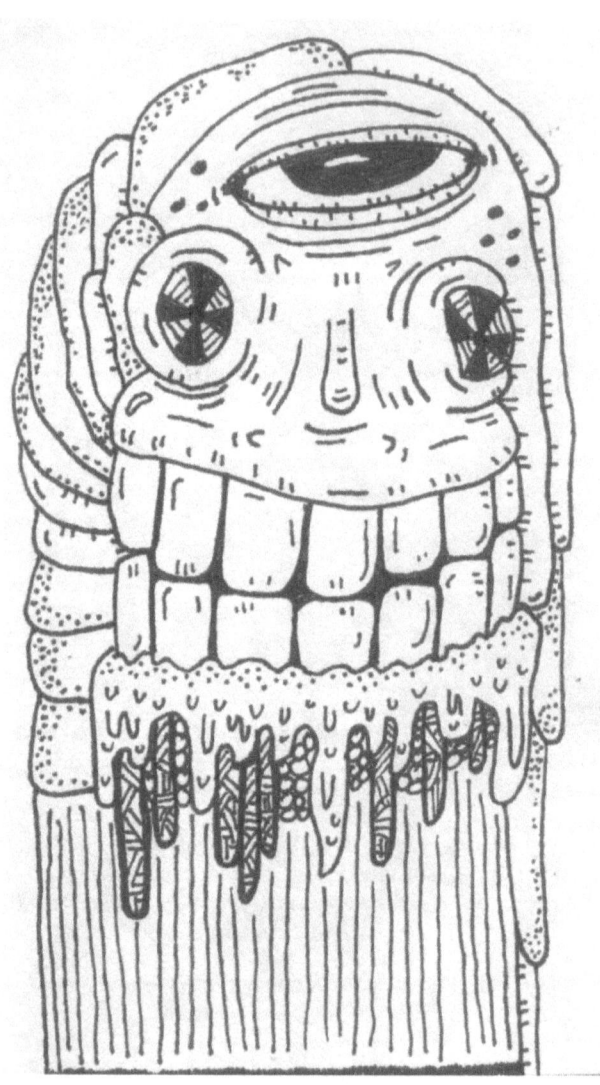

14

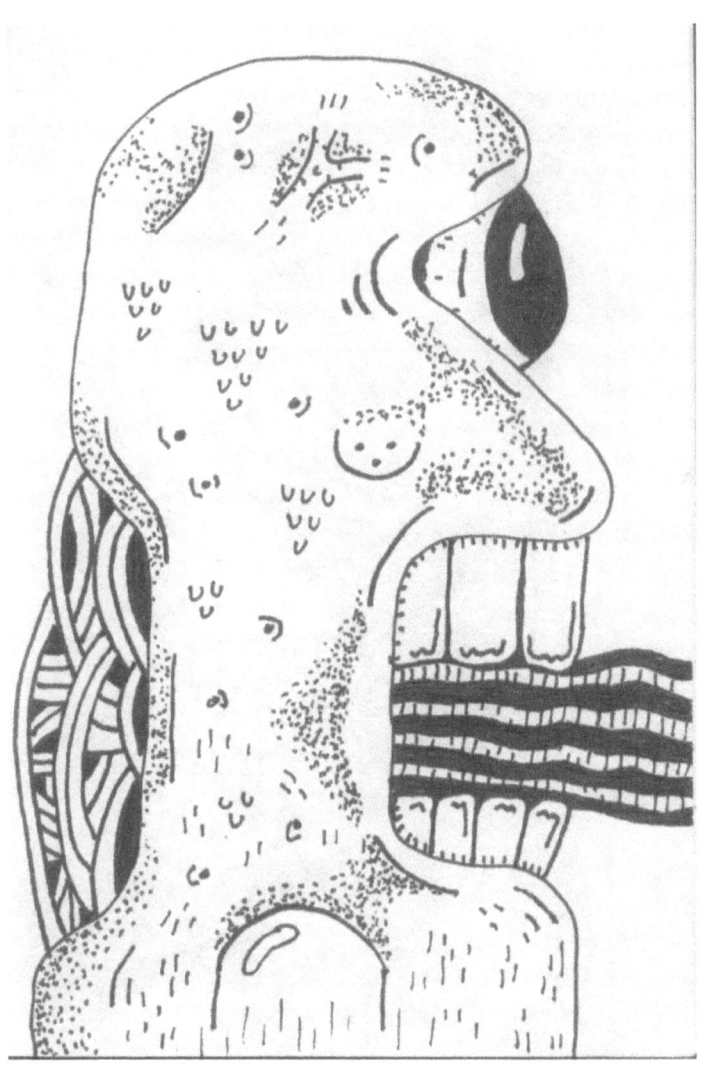

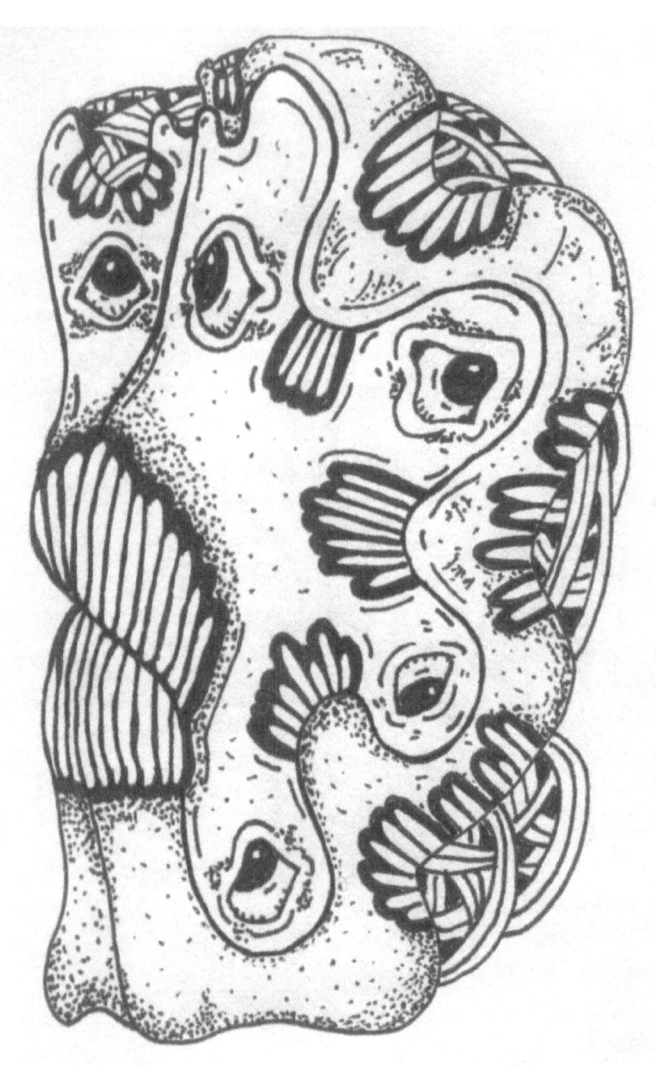

16

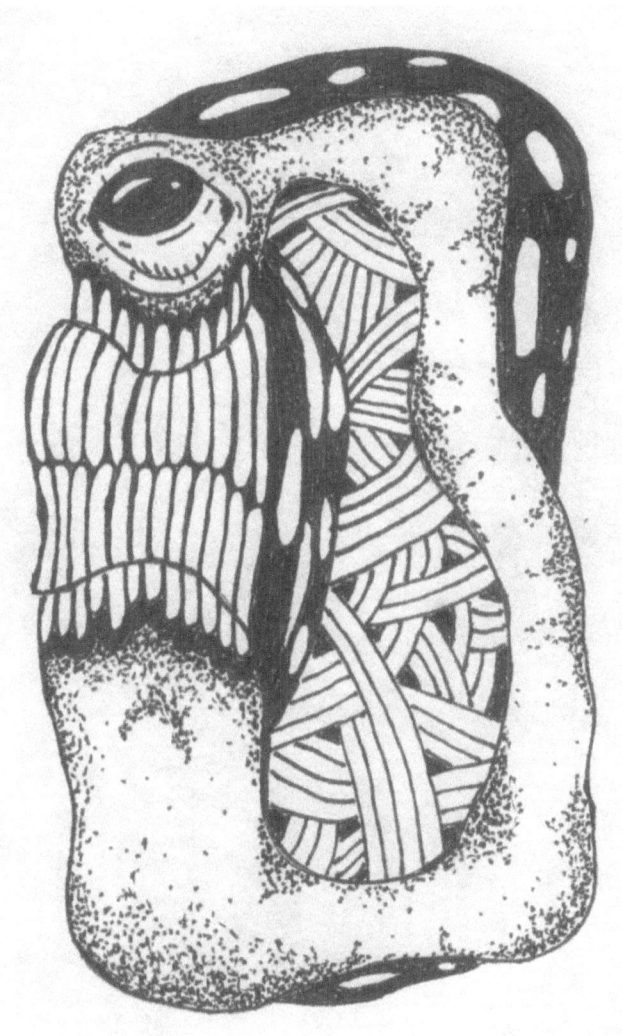

17

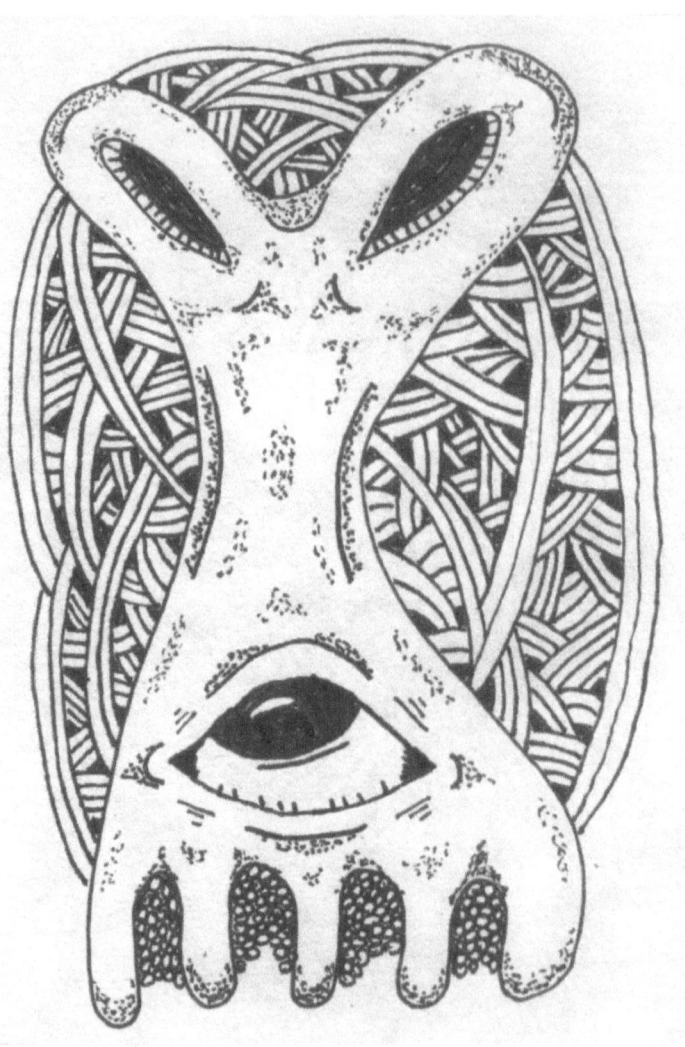

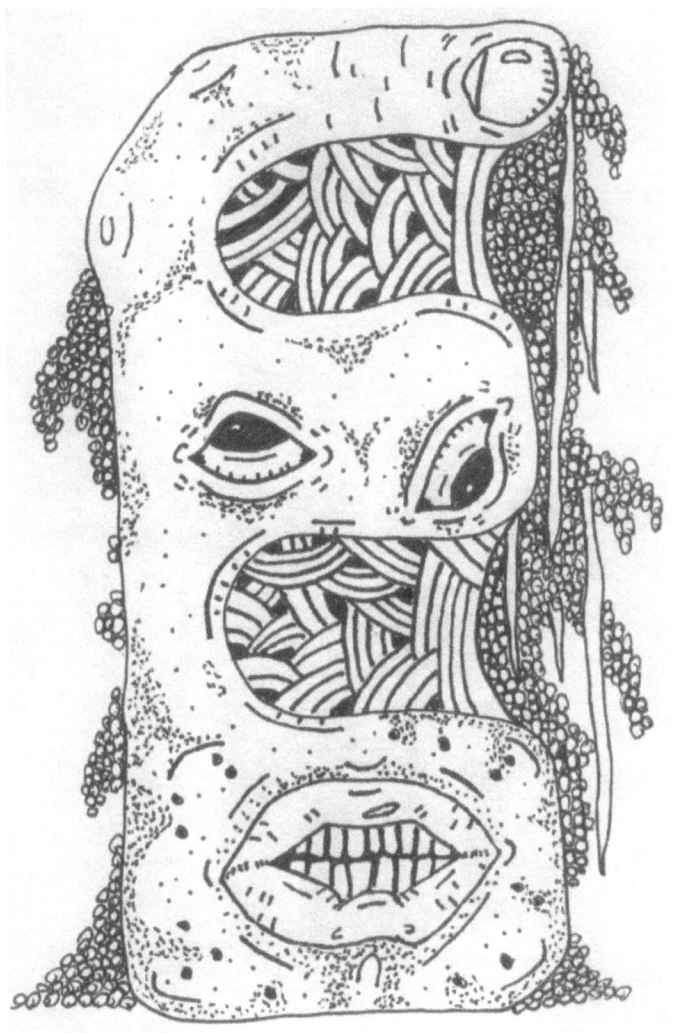

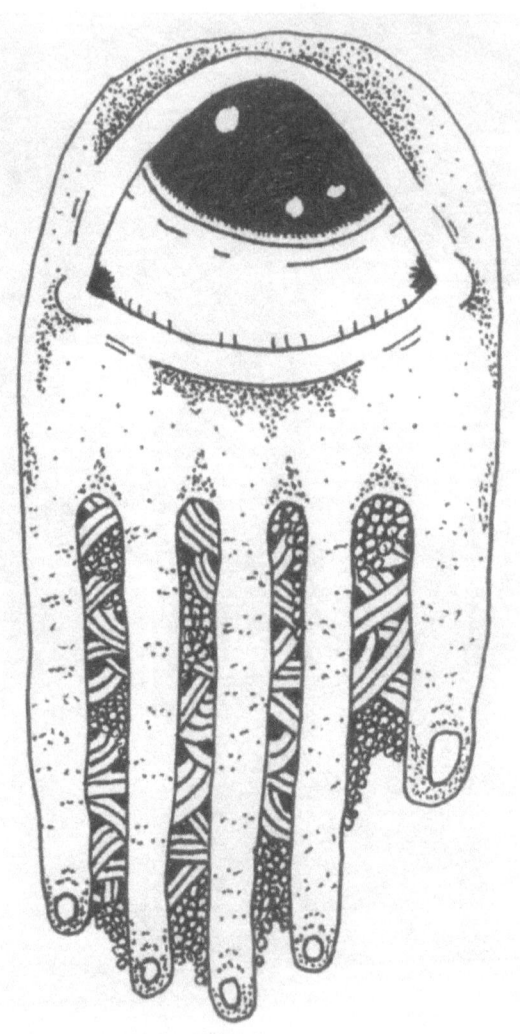

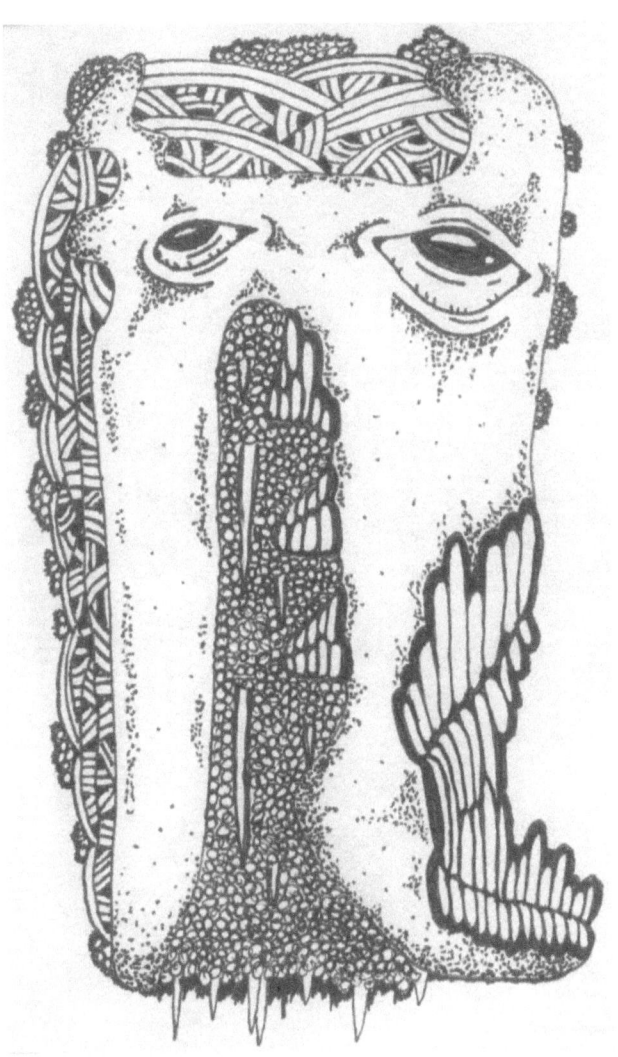

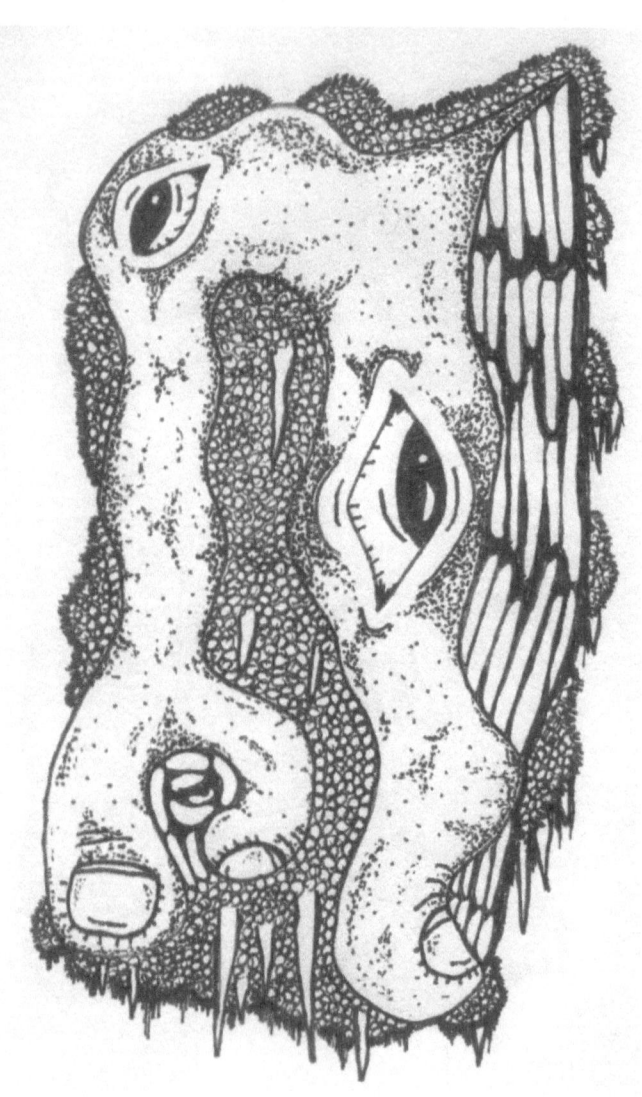

22

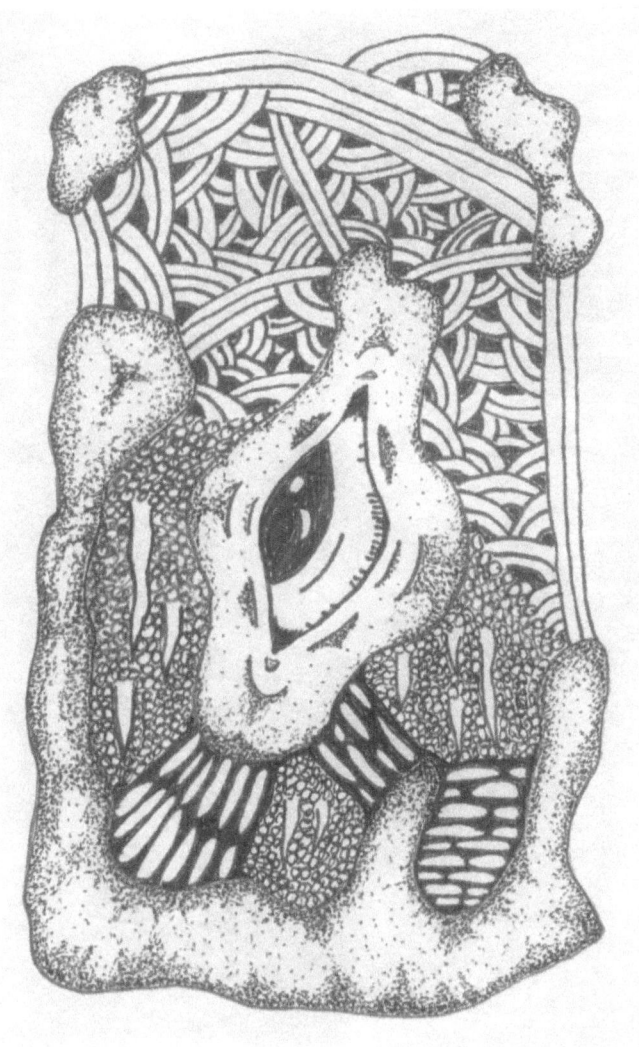

23

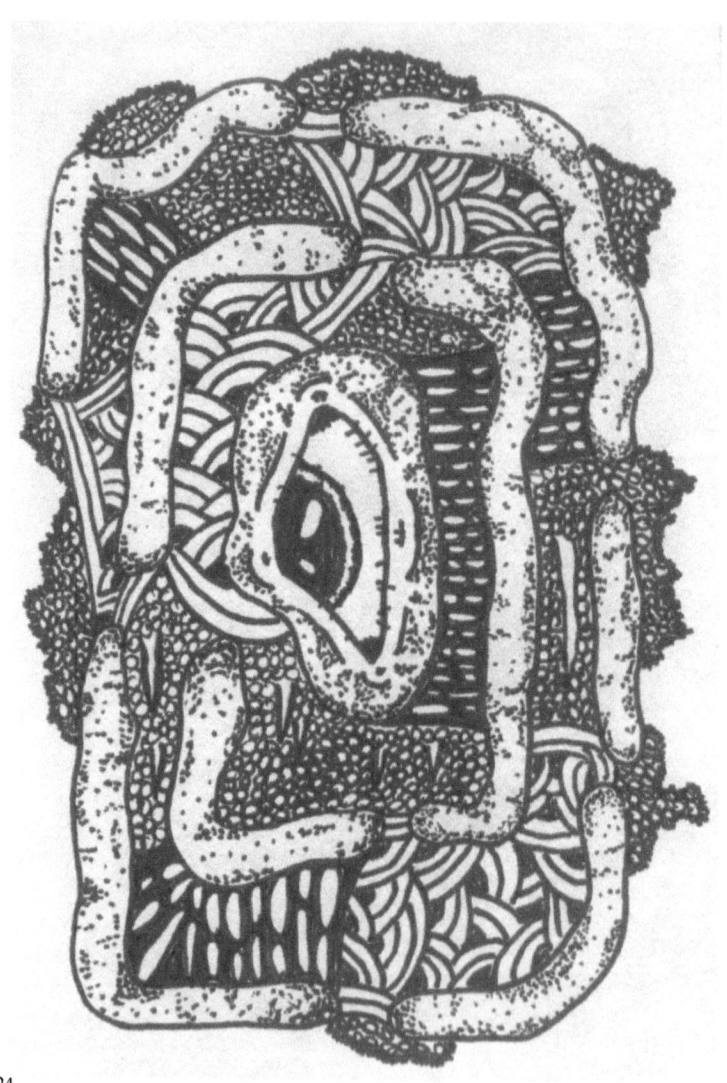

24

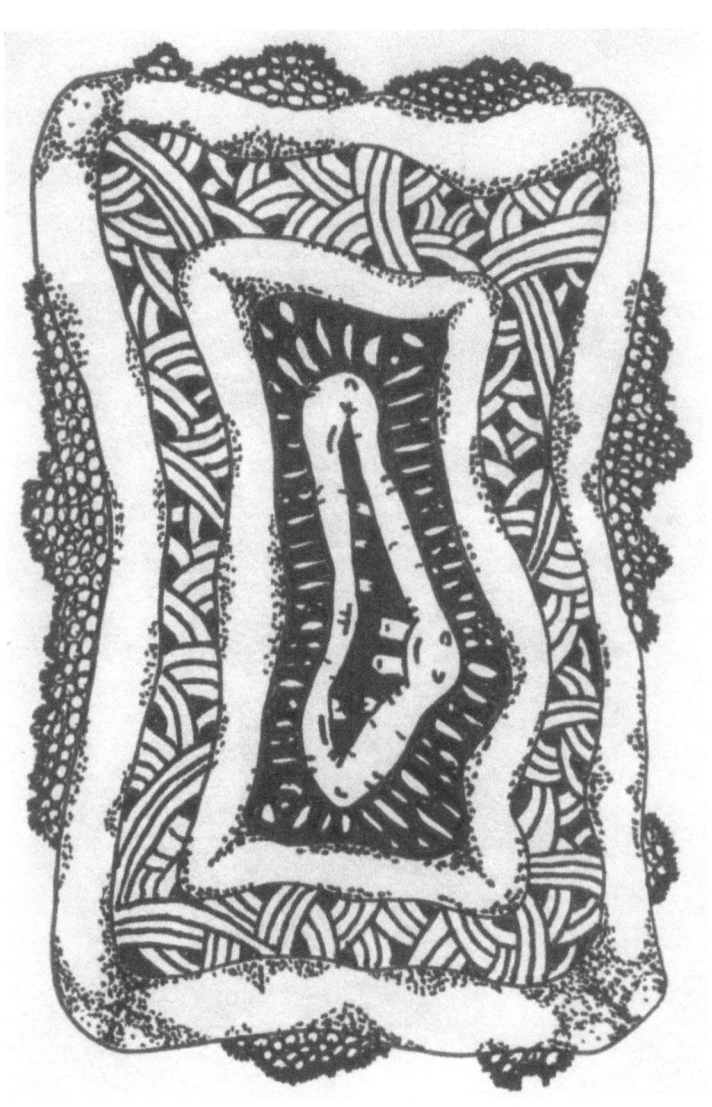

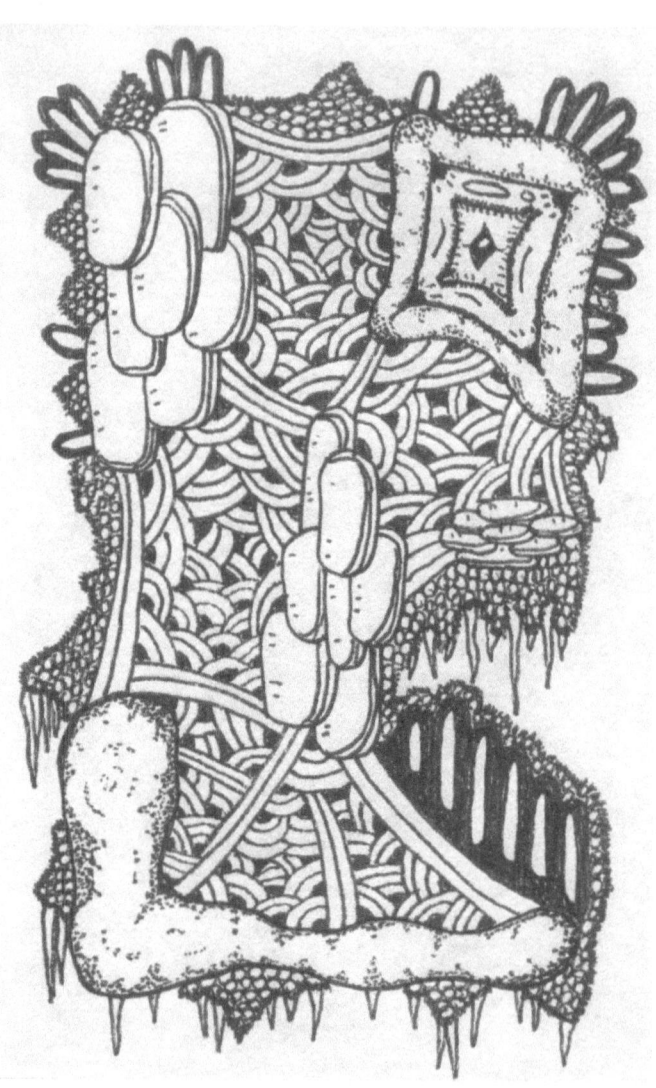

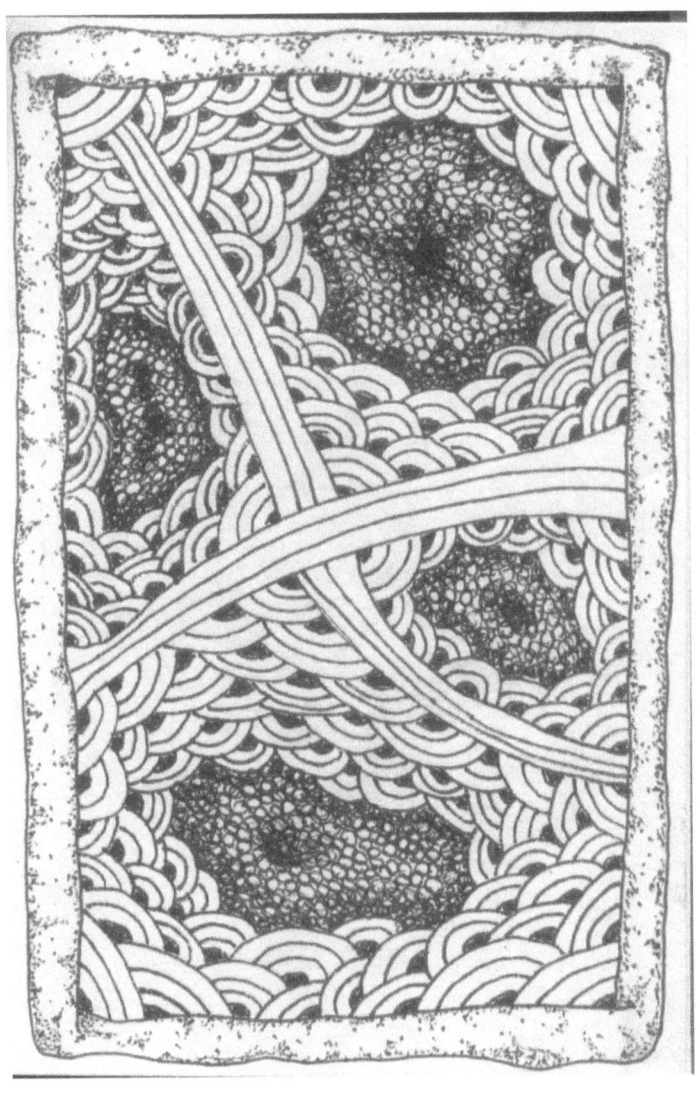

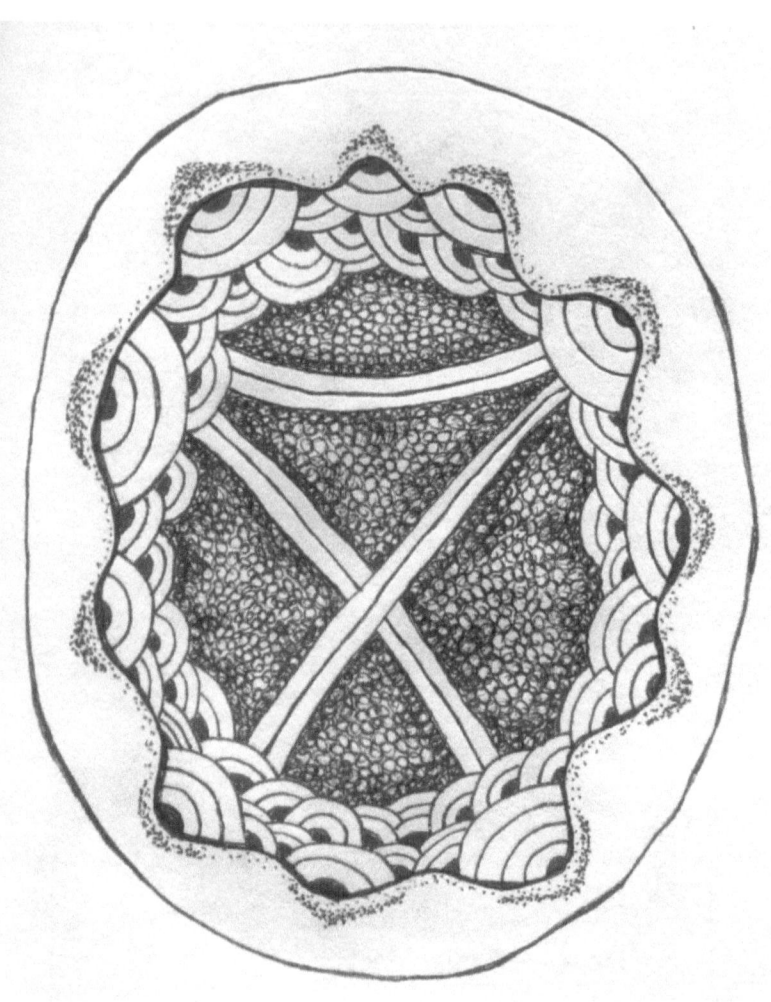

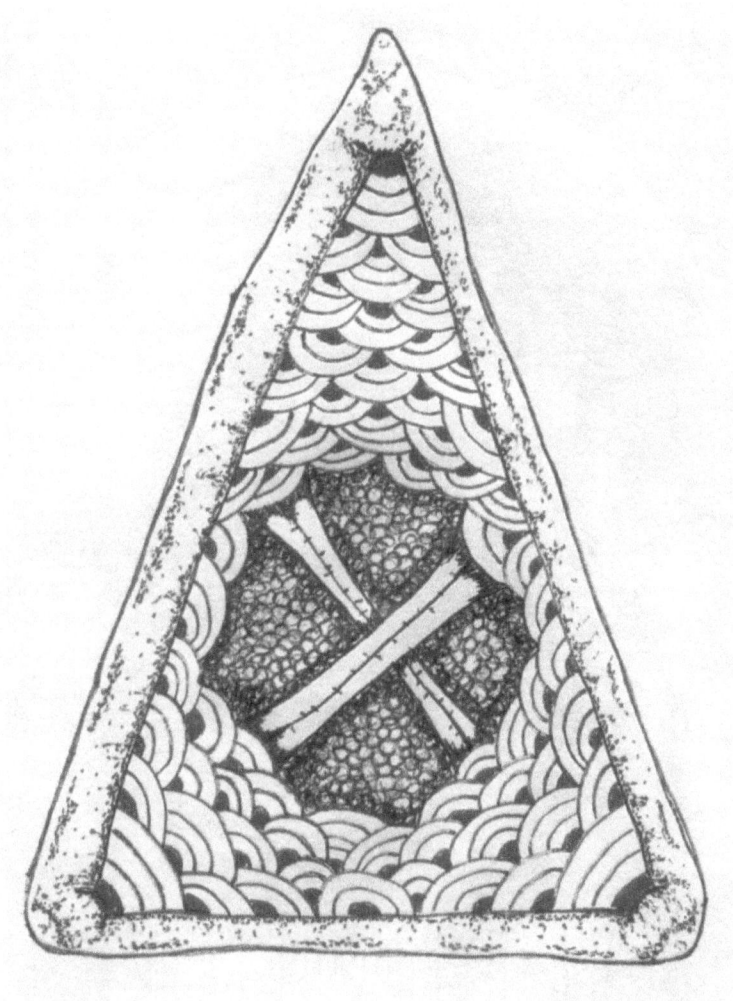

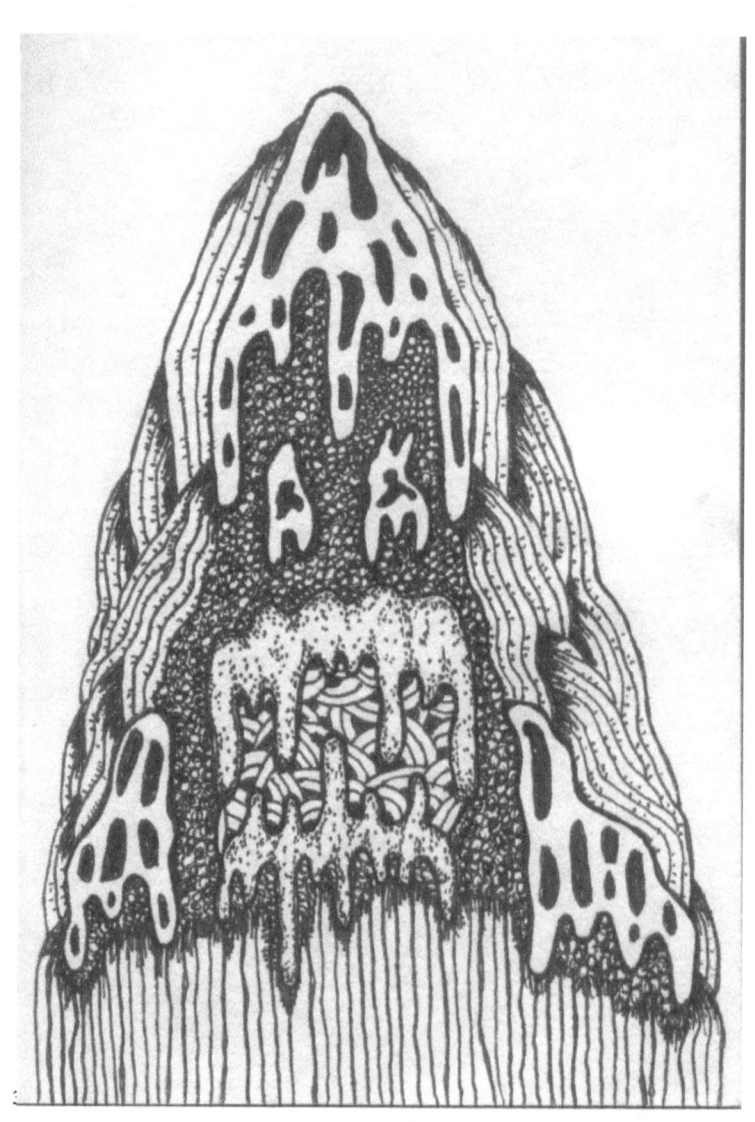

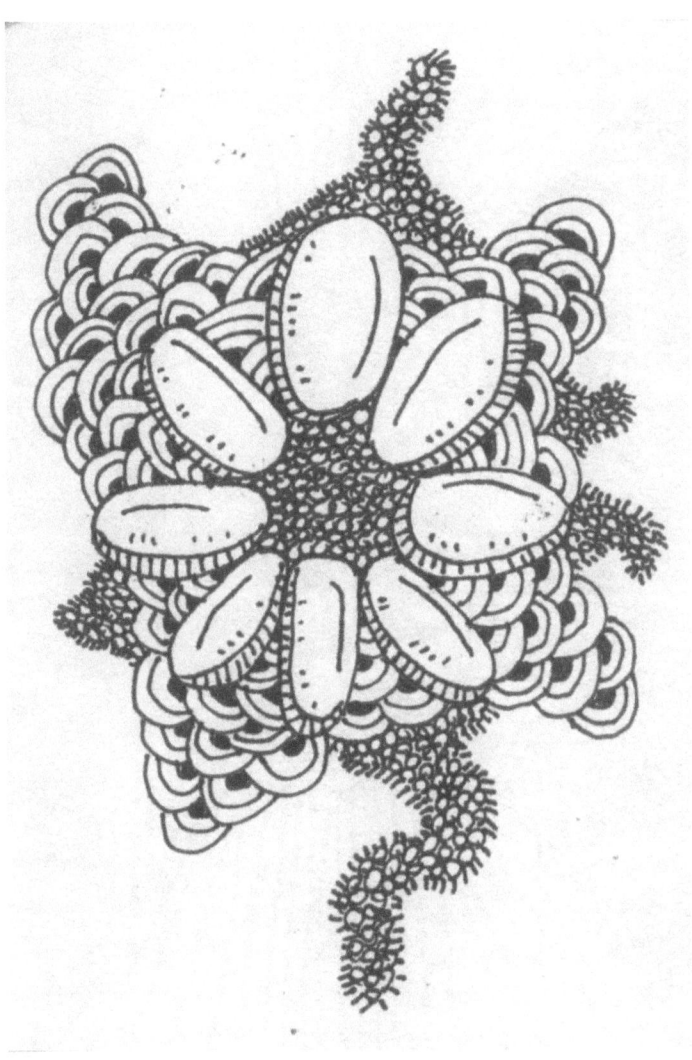

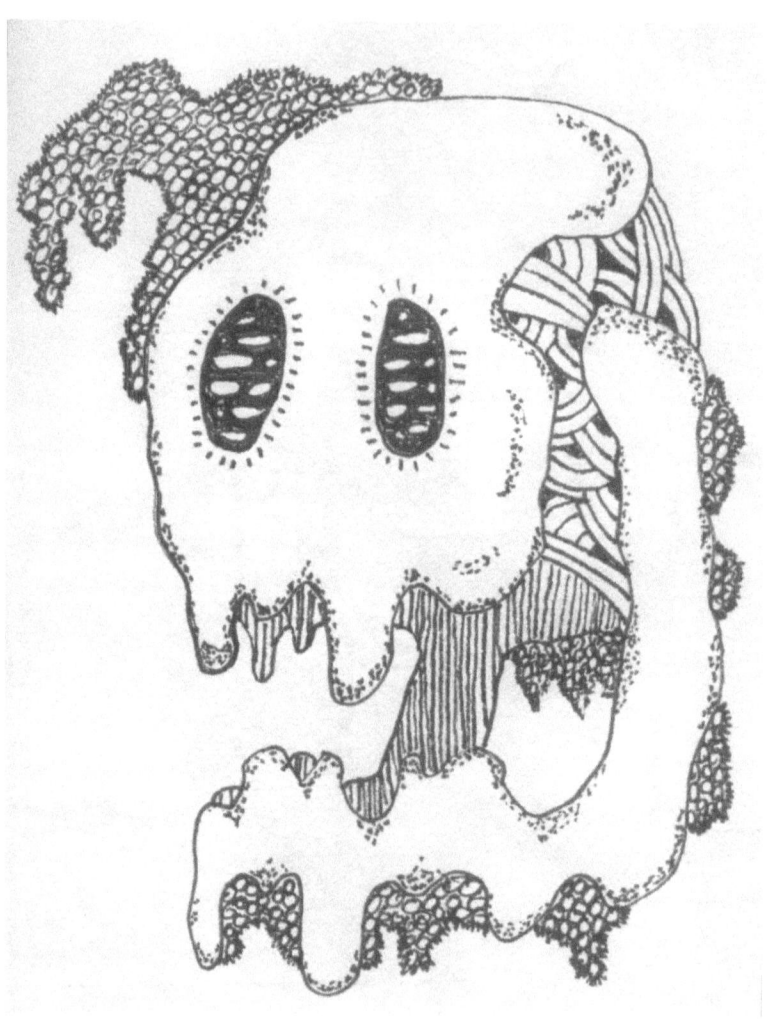

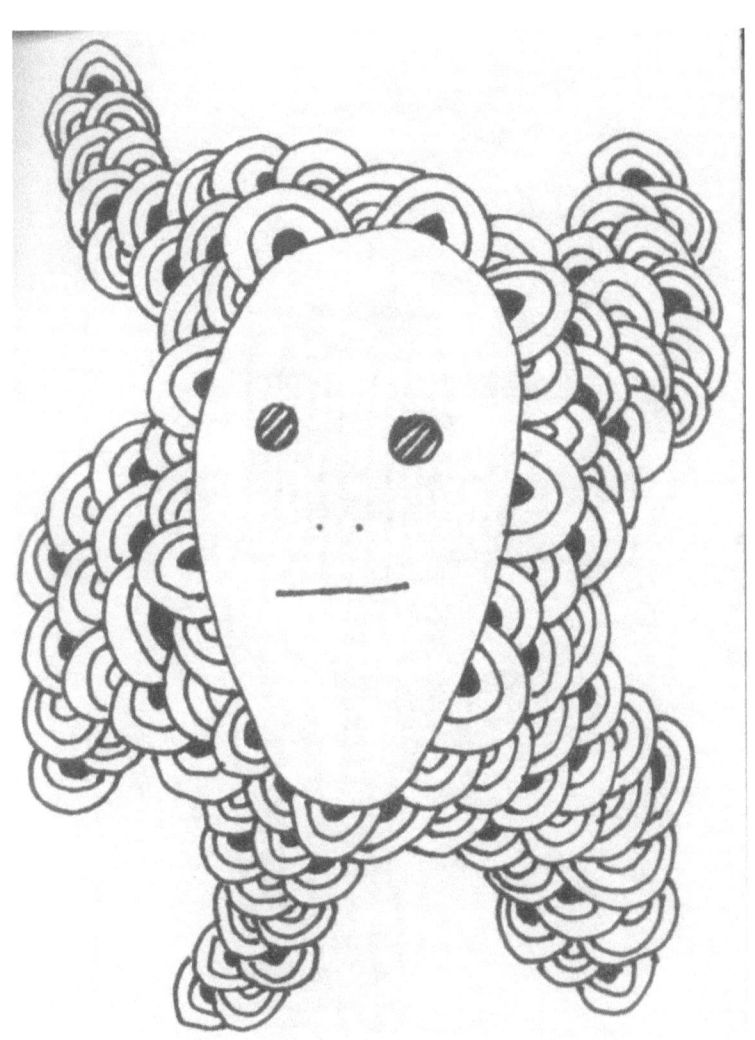

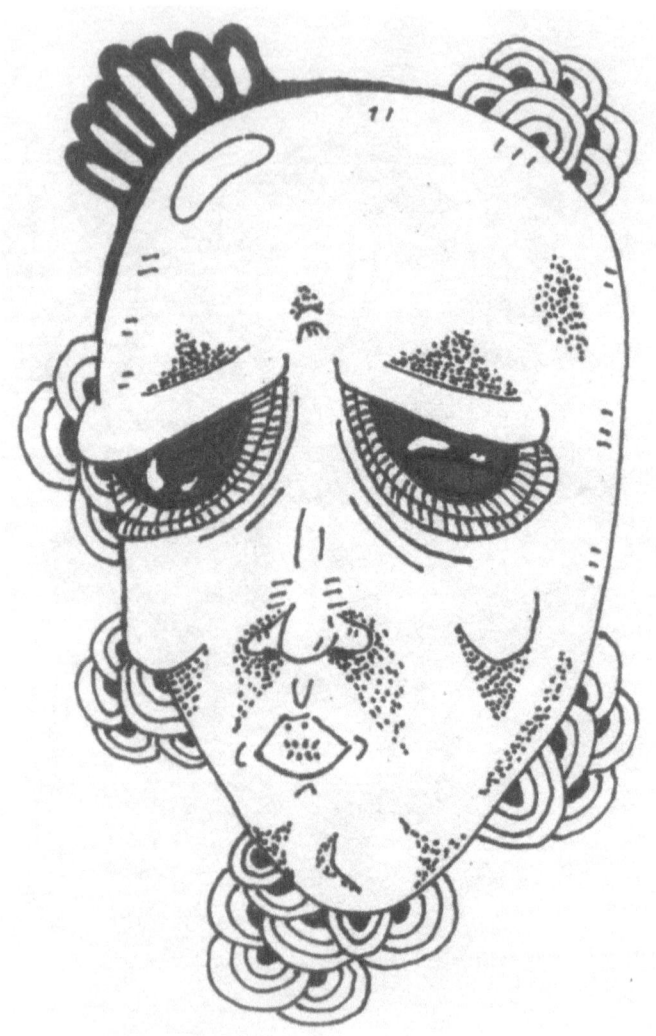

34

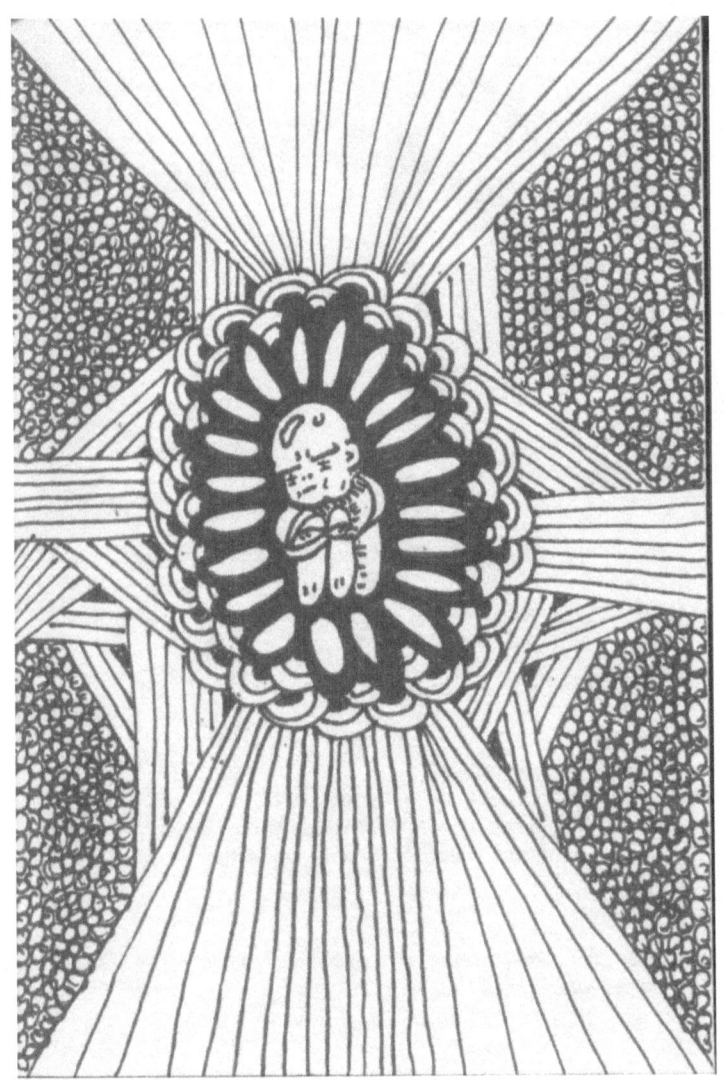

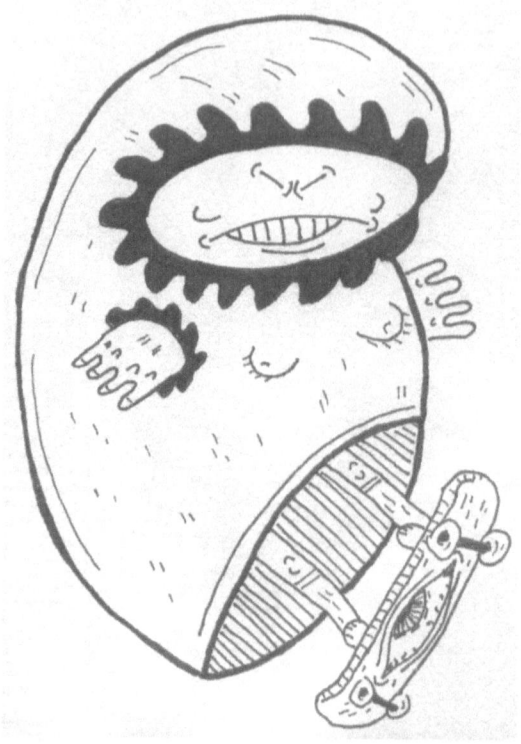

These final sketches are all very different in context. I did what
I could to keep drawing something different, adding
something new, or trying something new.

have filled 3-4 sketchbooks, and most of these final pictures were
dated and titled, but for no real purpose other than
documentation of time and my thoughts.

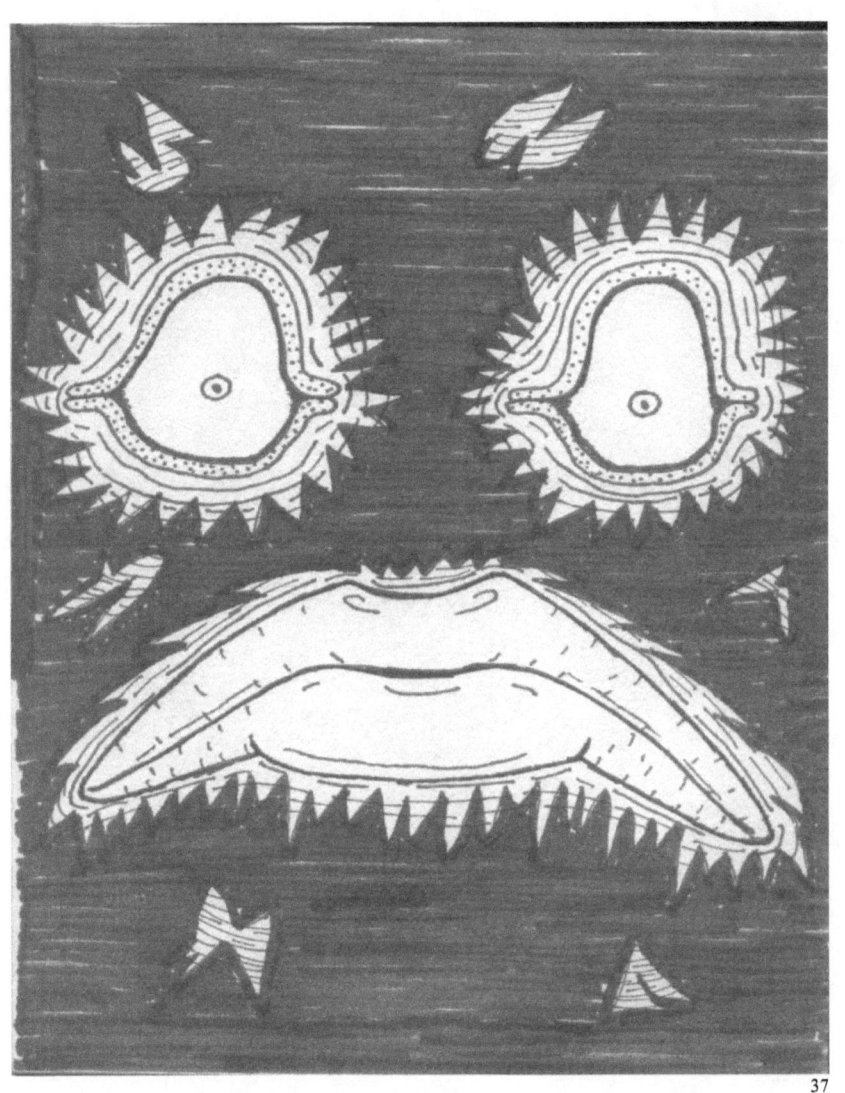

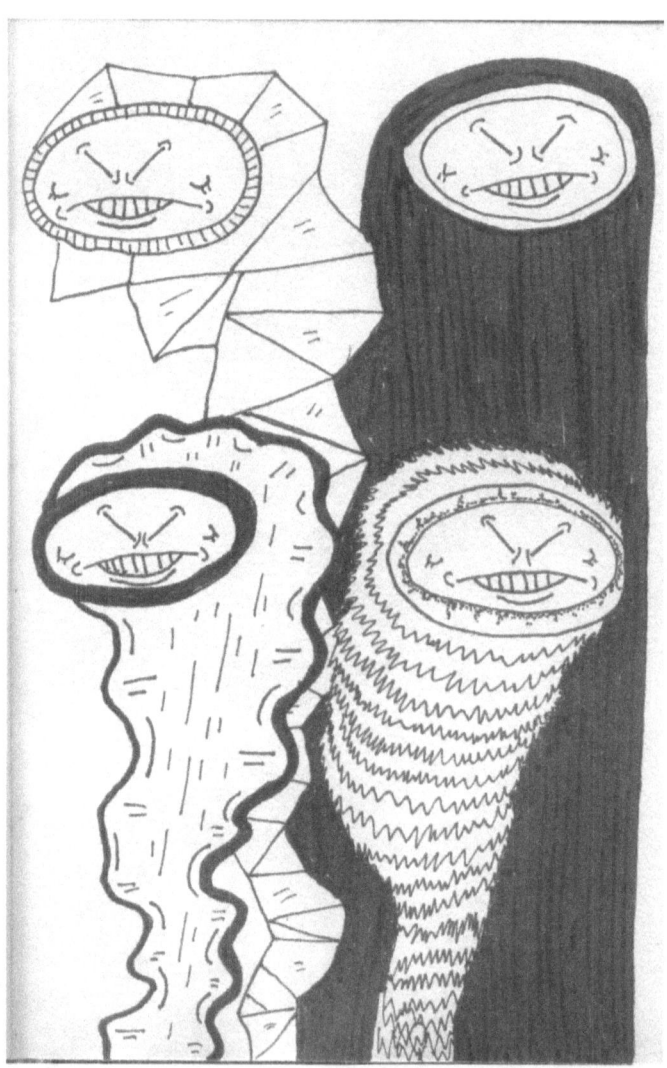

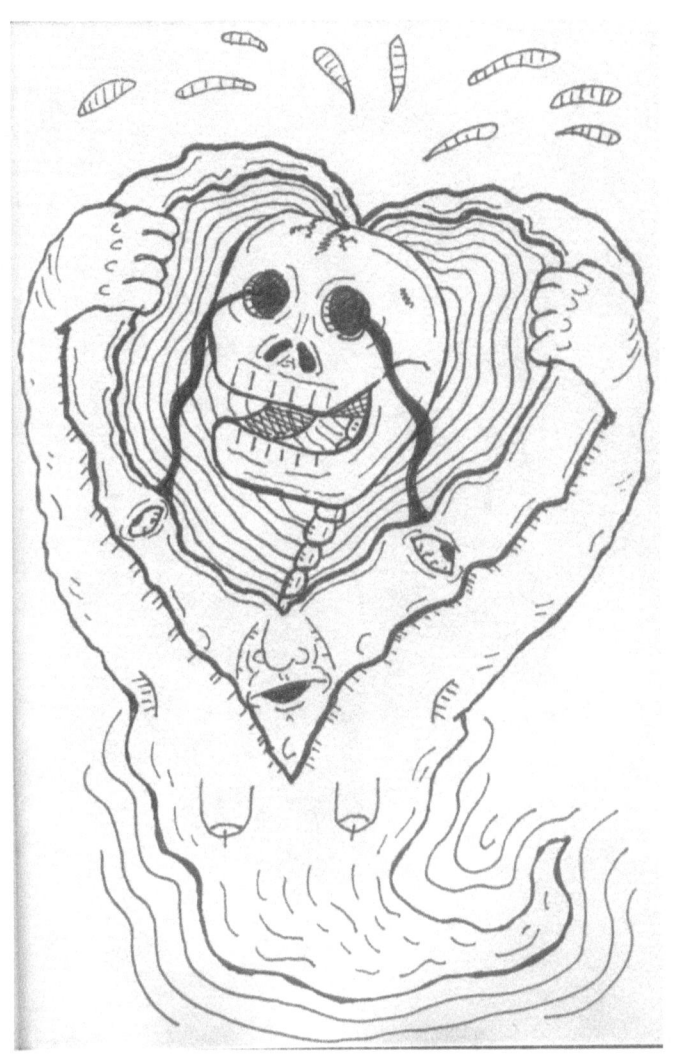

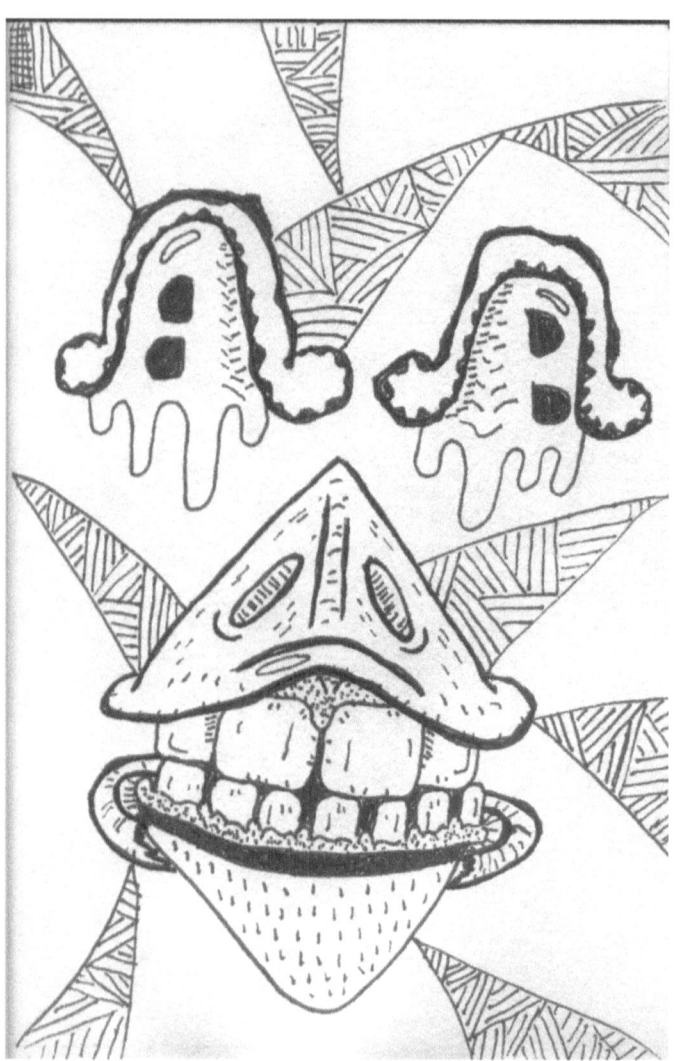

40

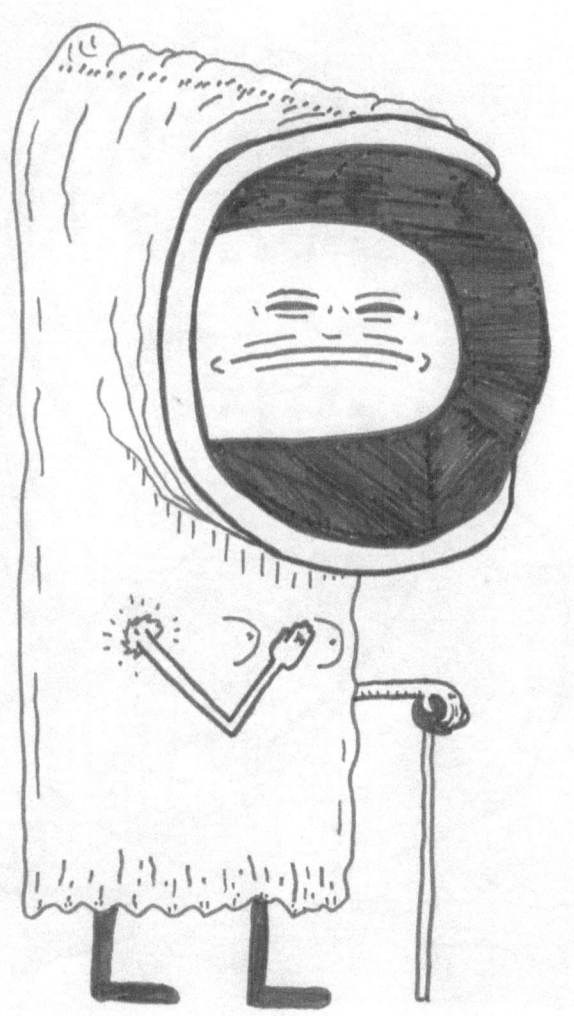

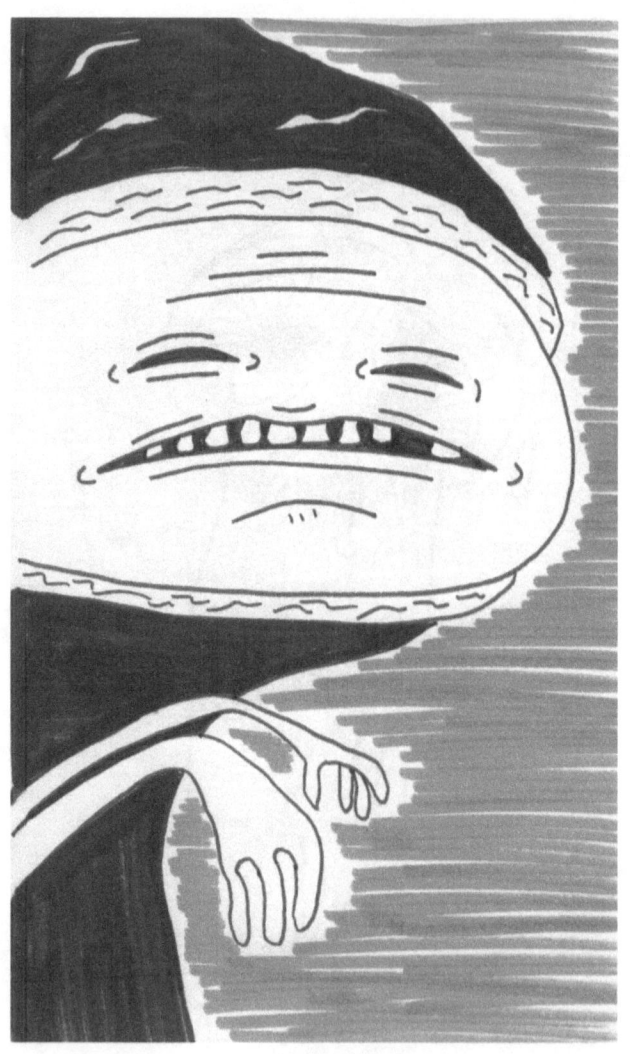

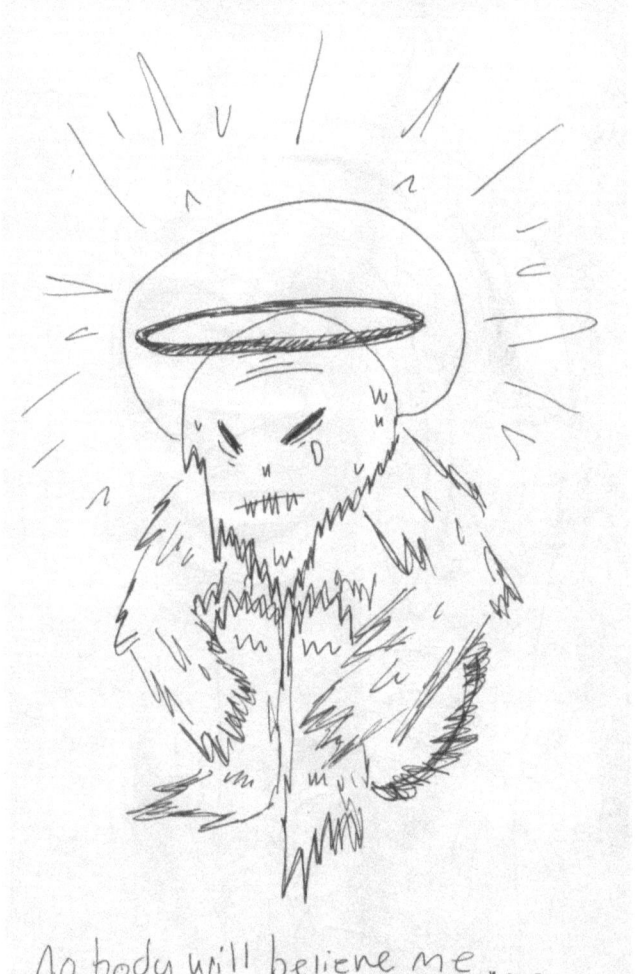

No body will believe me ...

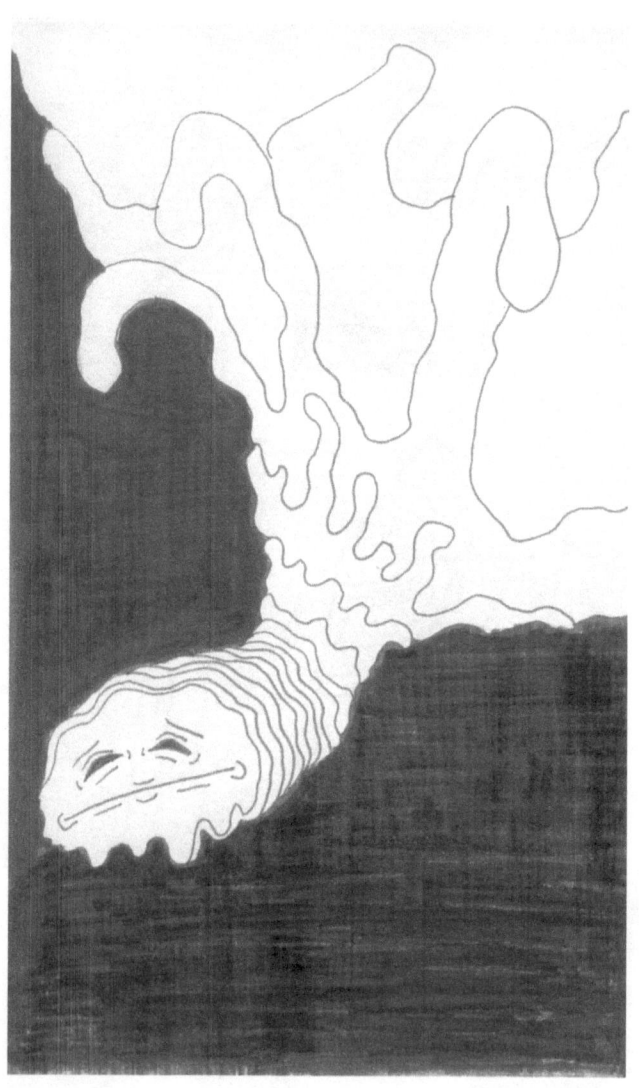

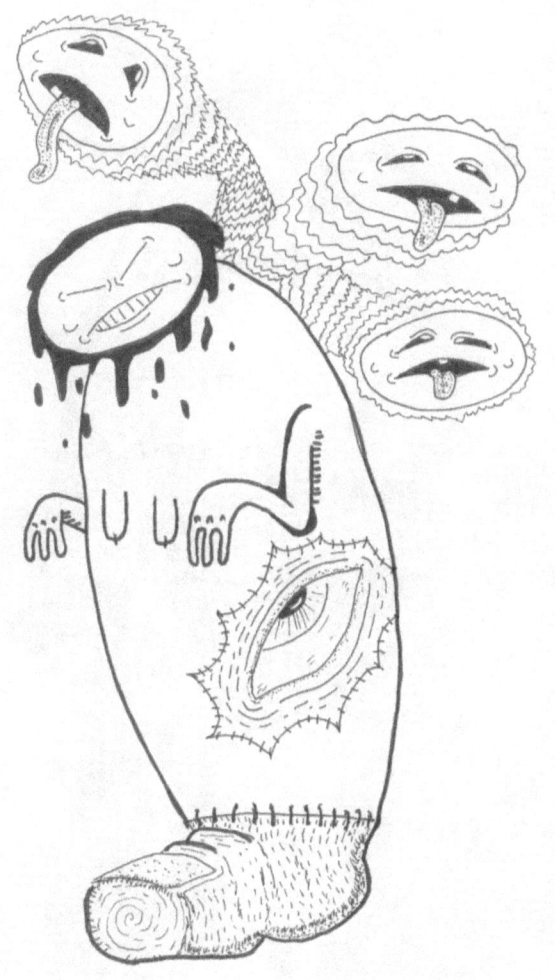

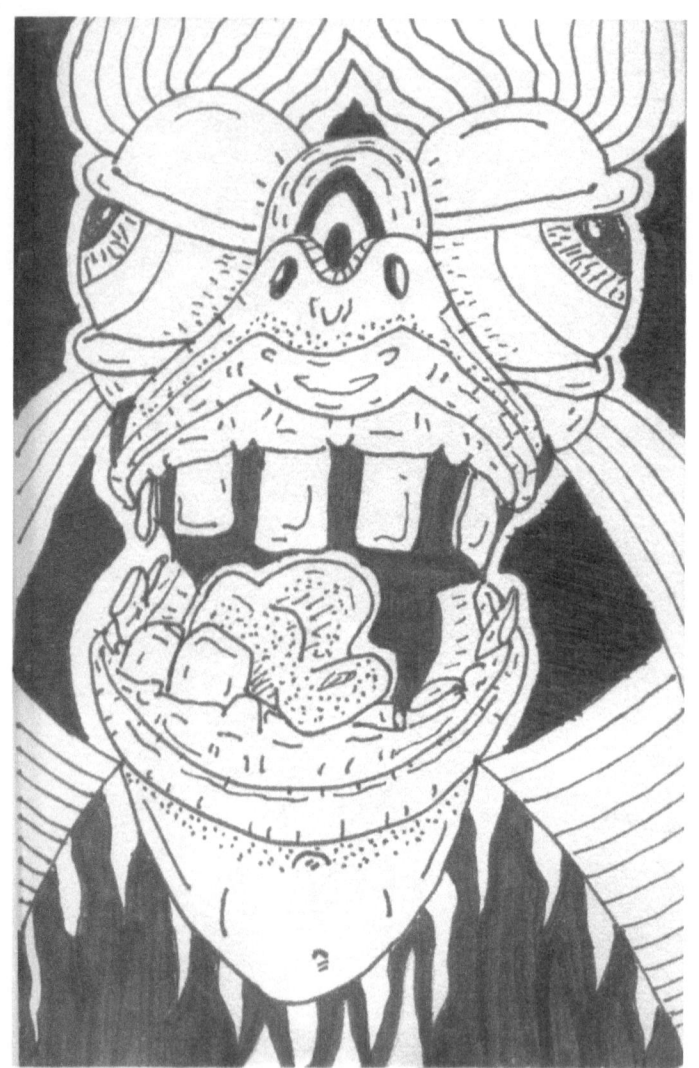

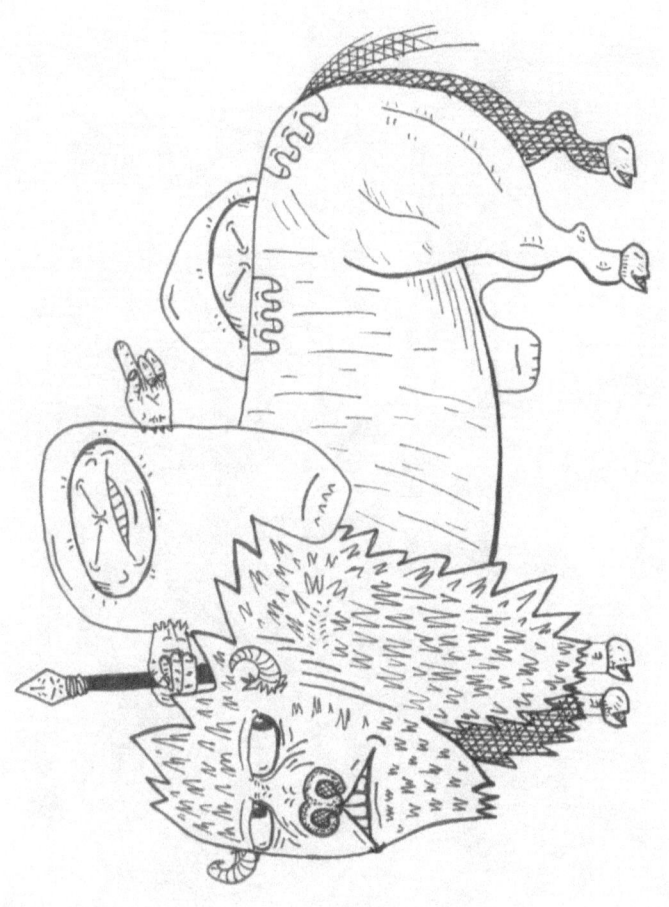

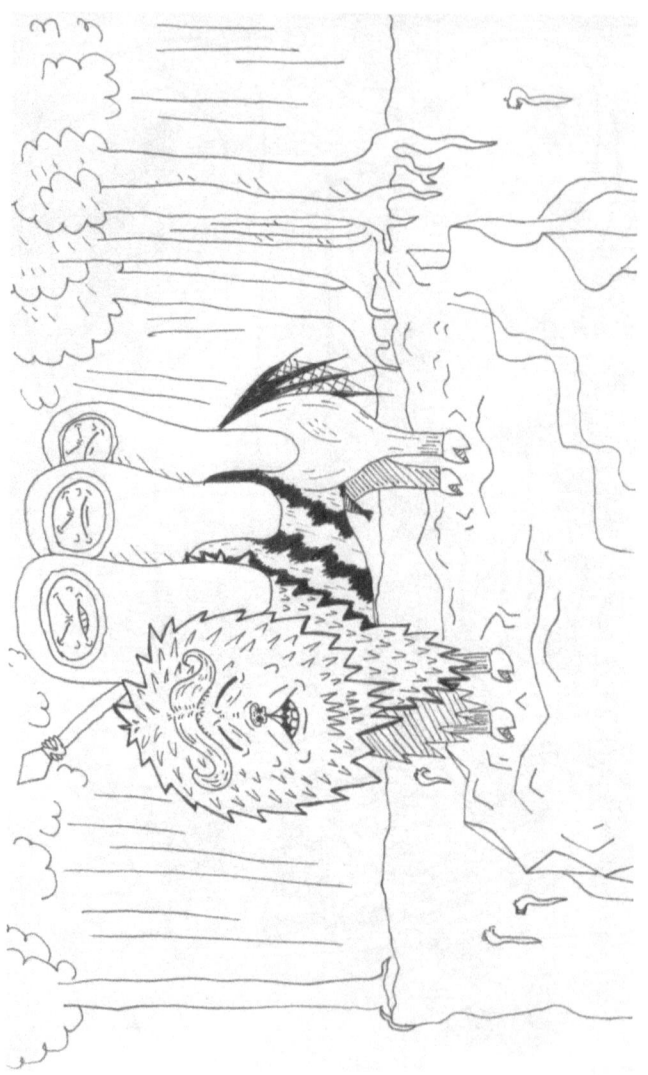

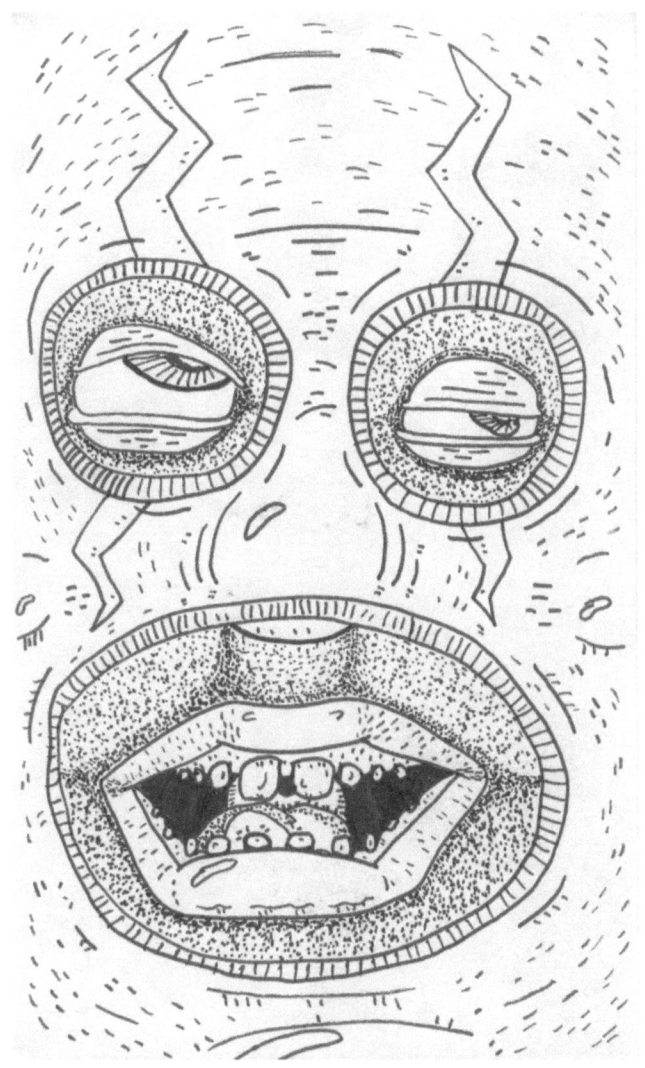

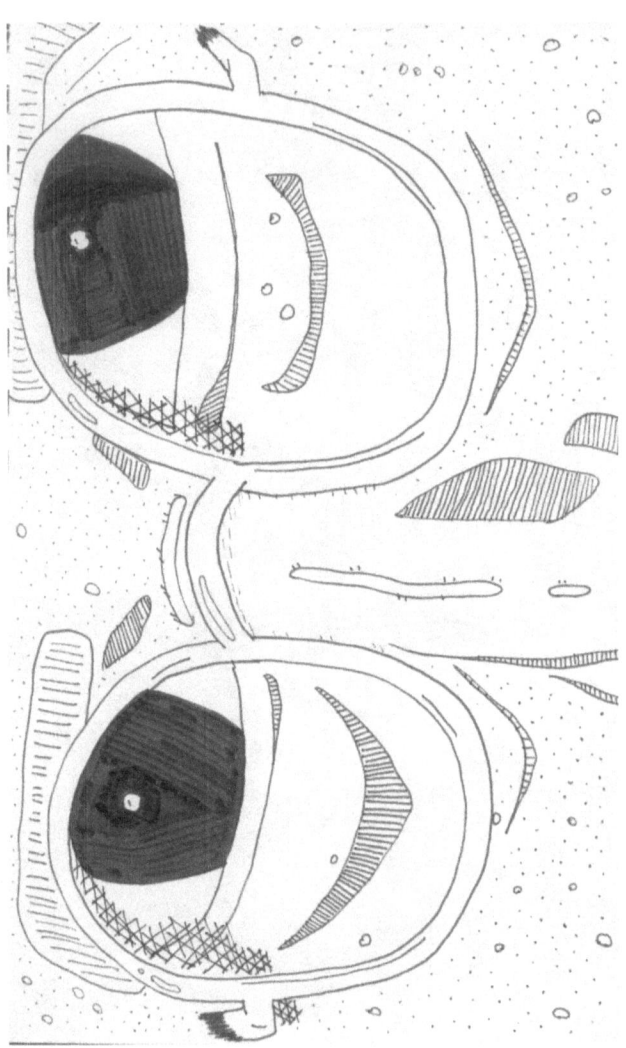

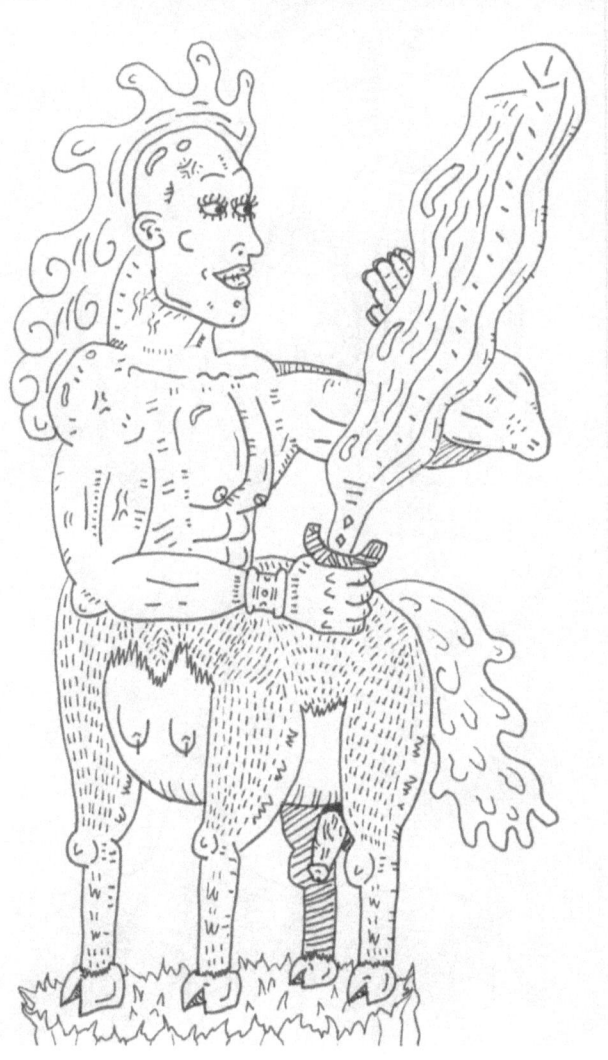

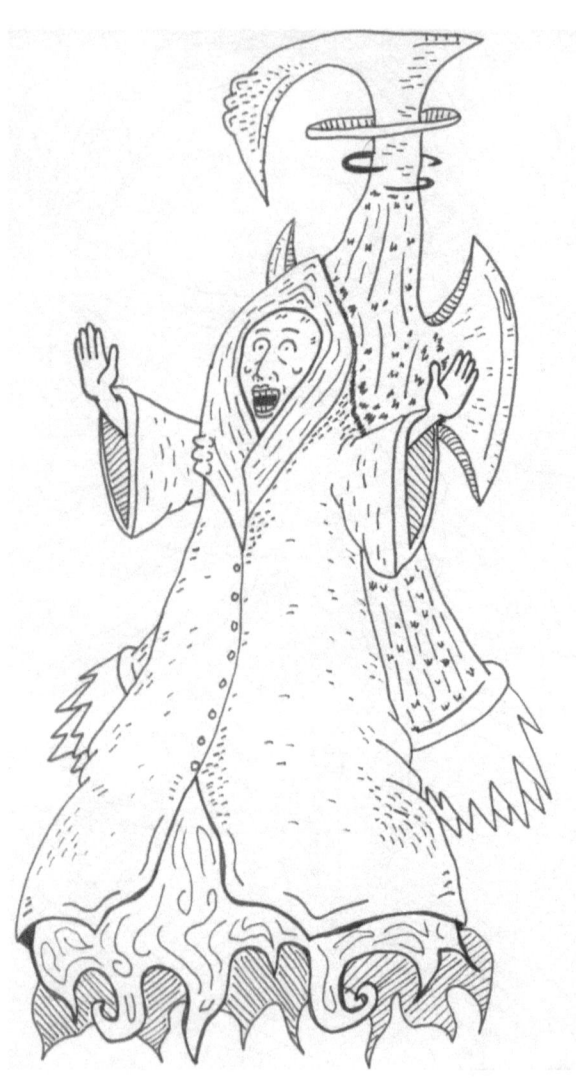

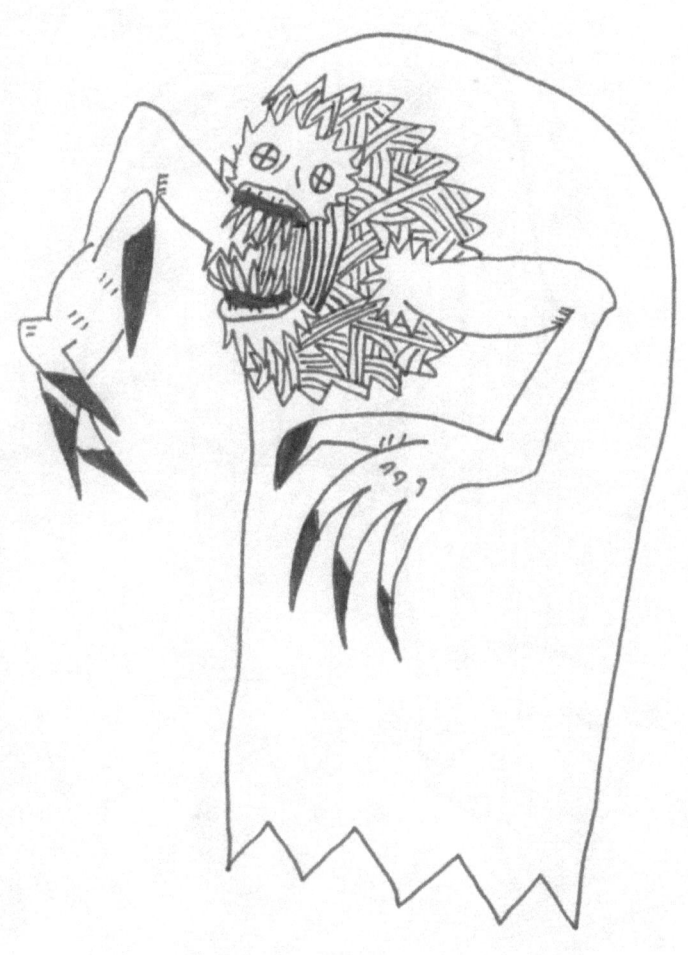

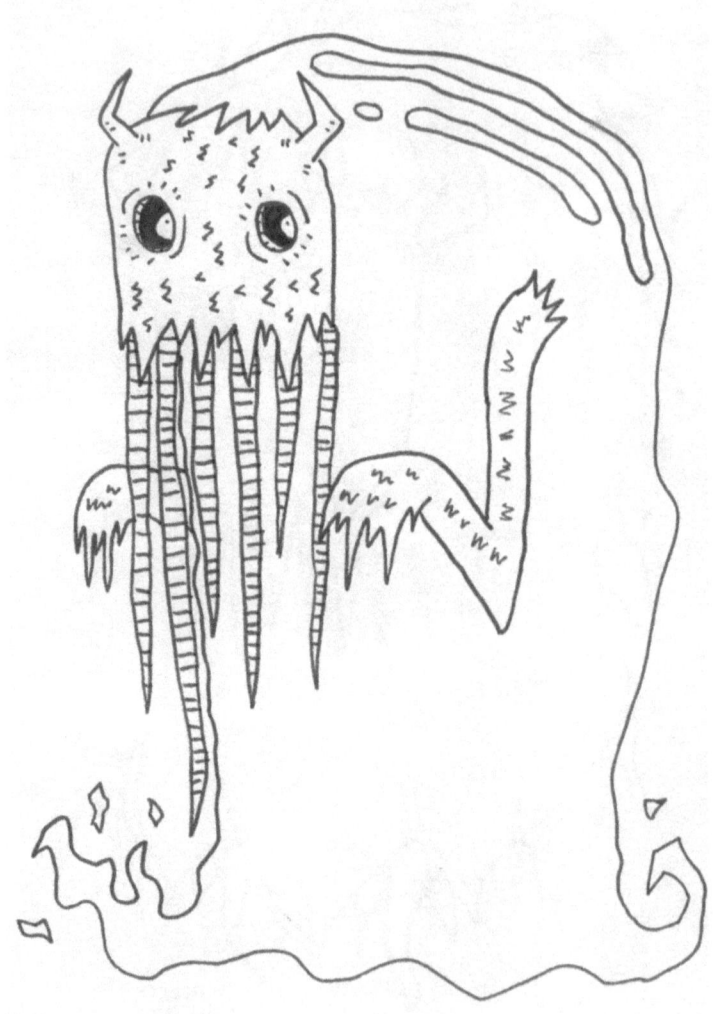

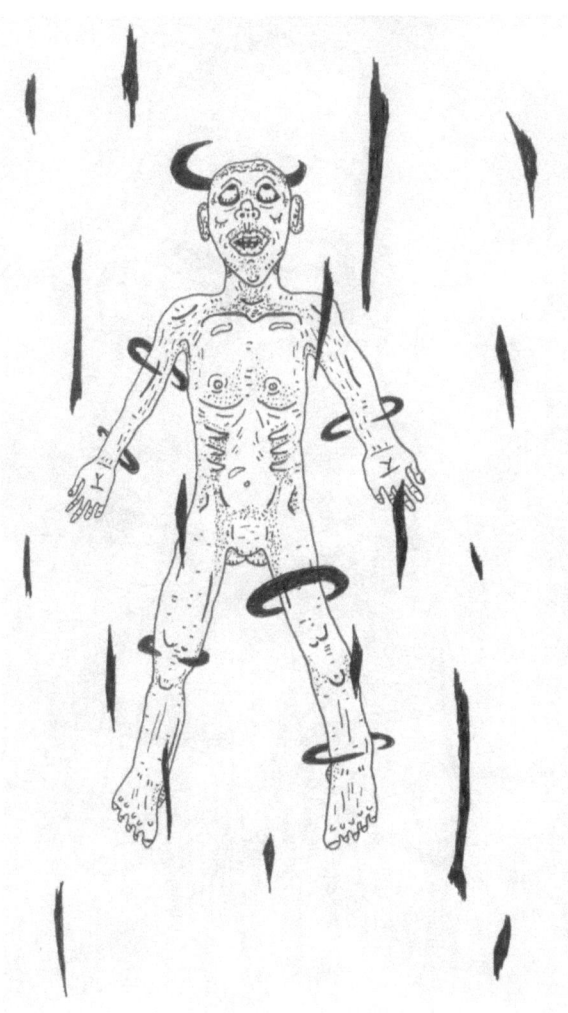

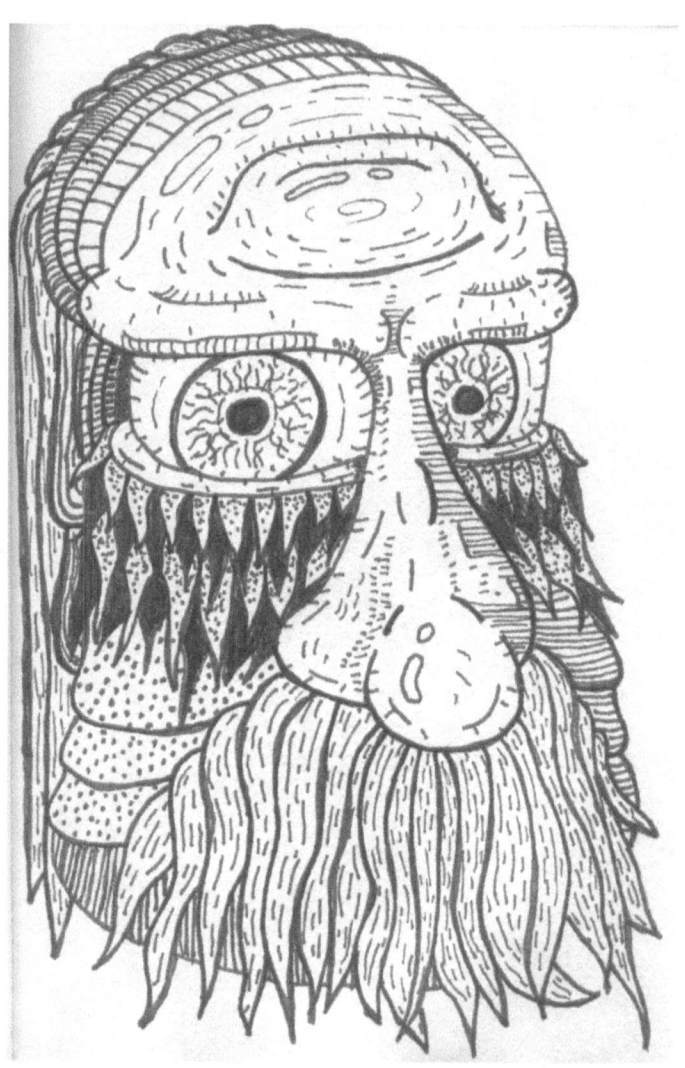

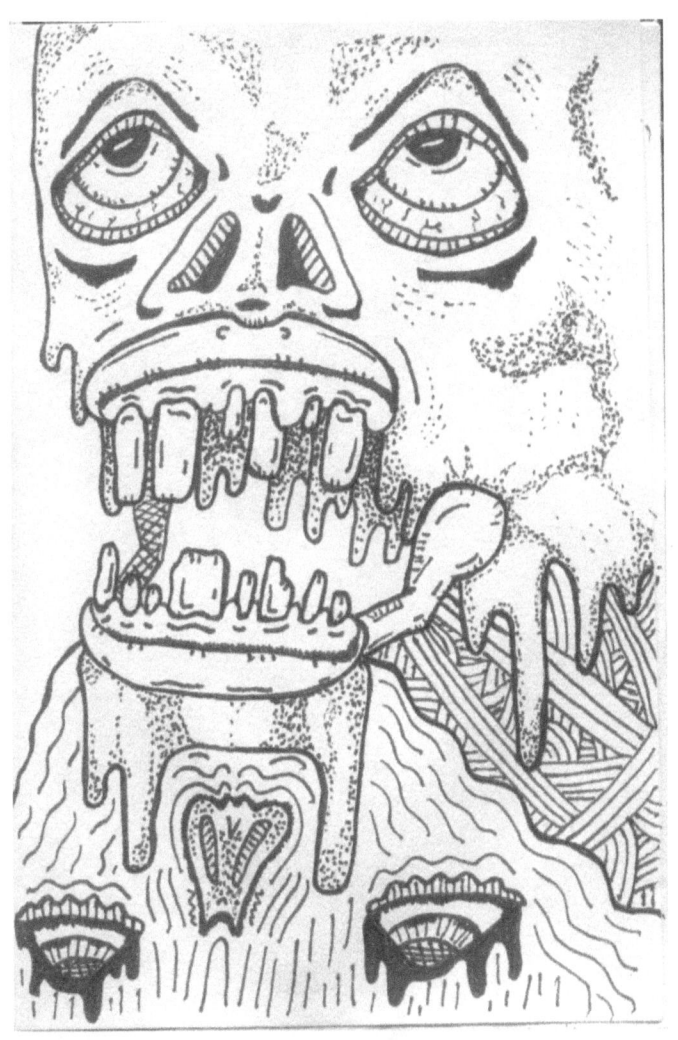

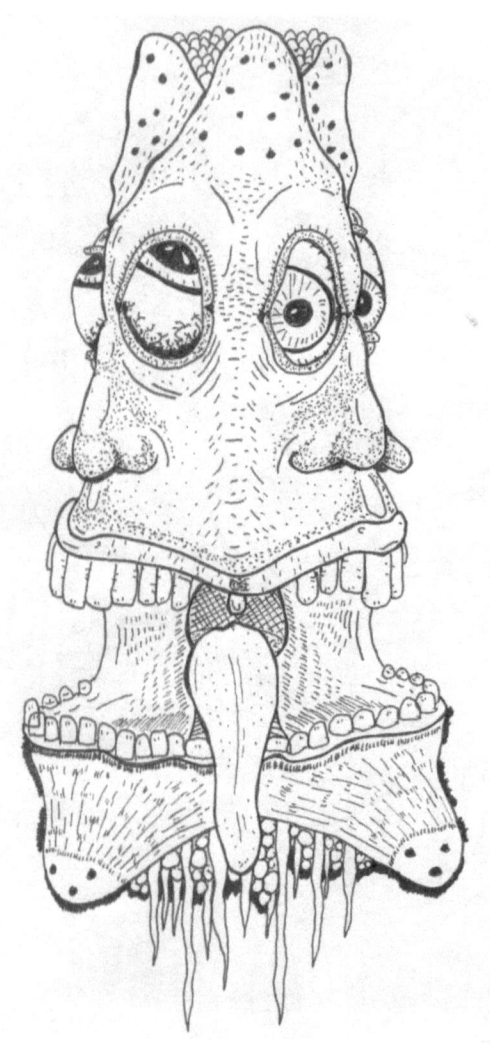

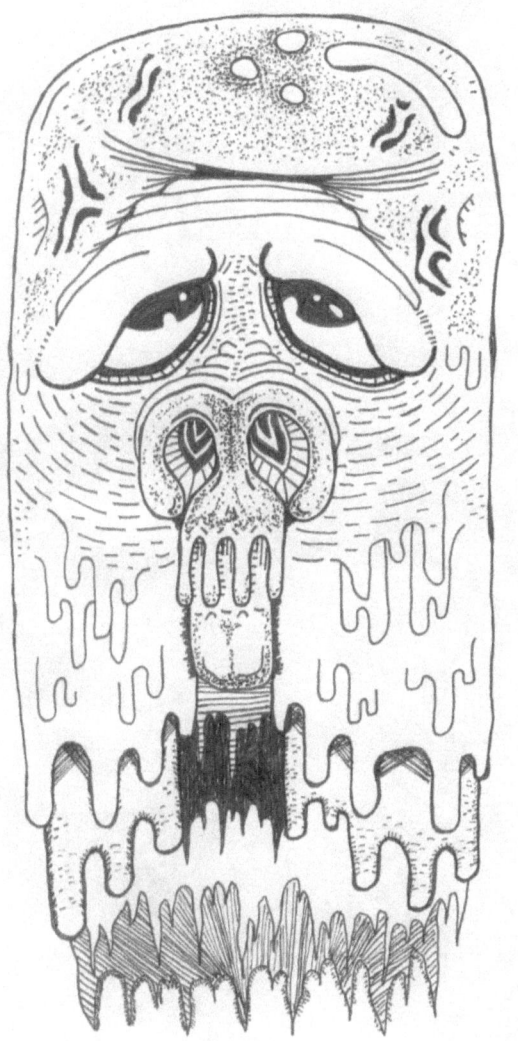

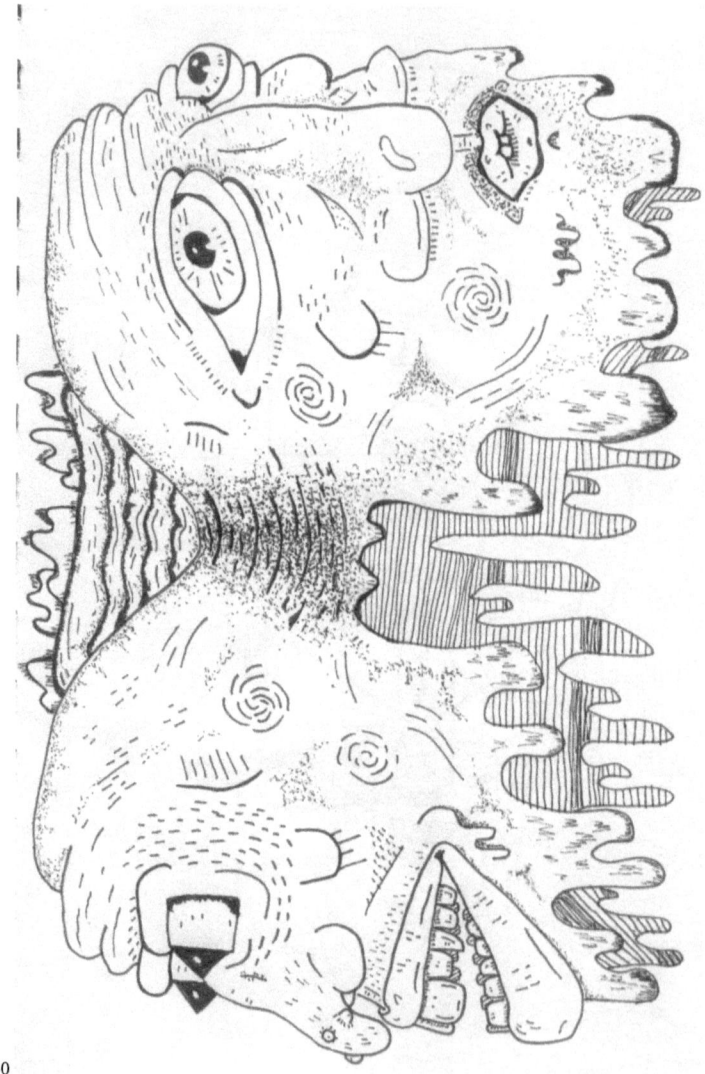

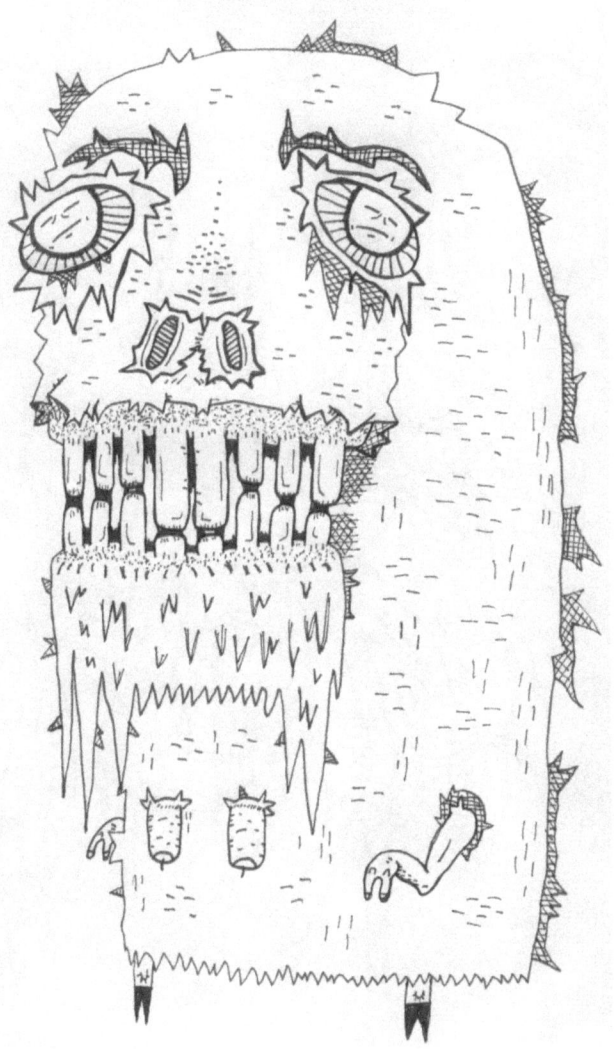

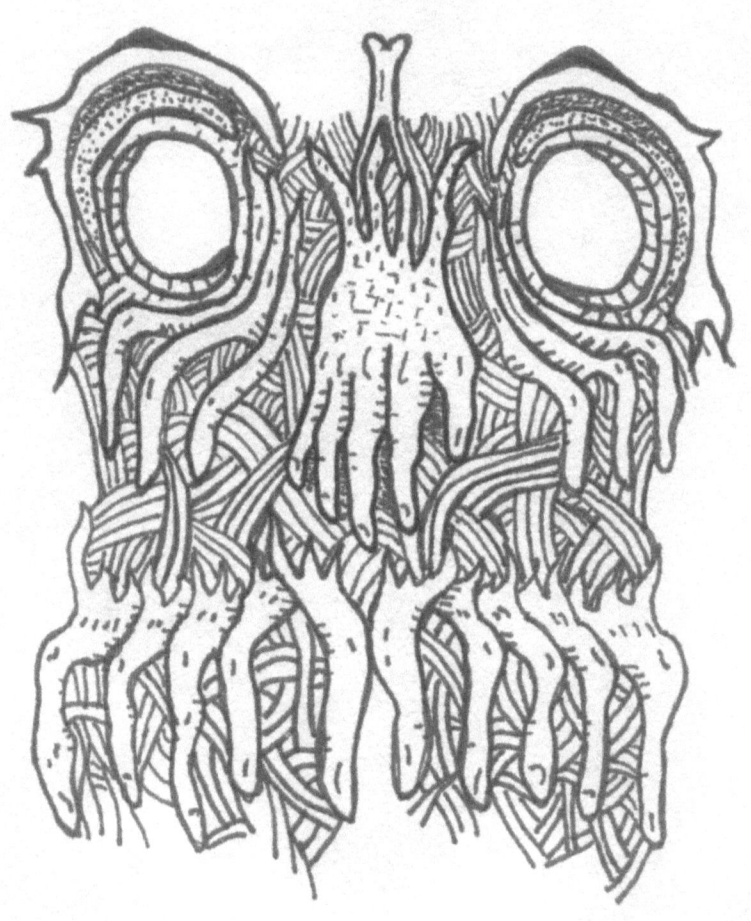

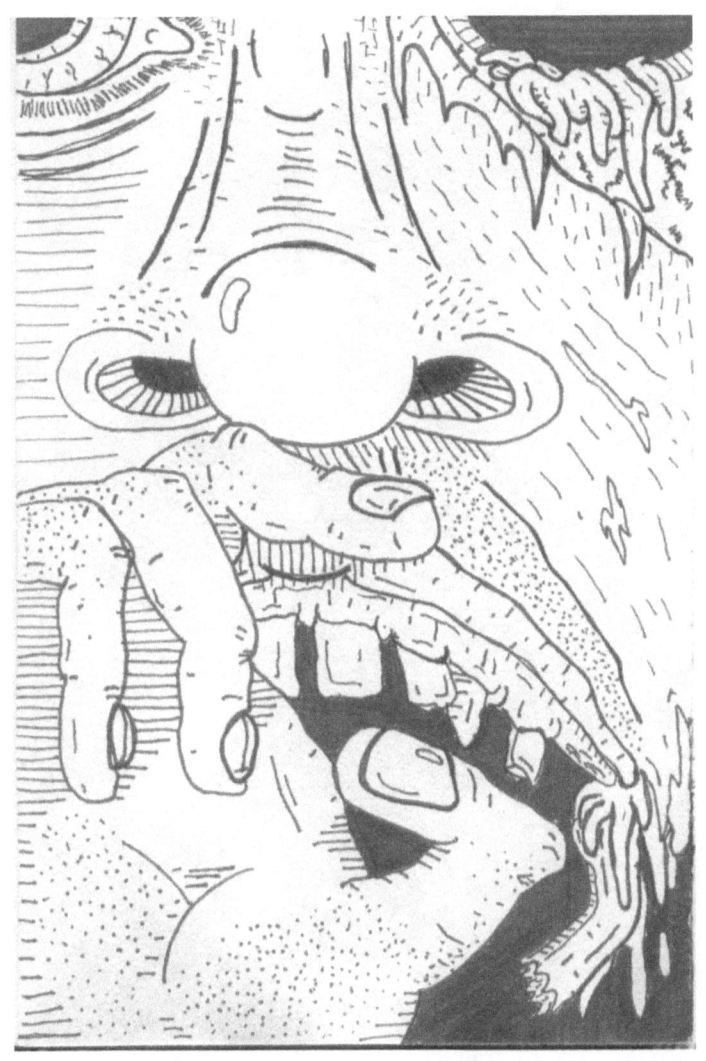

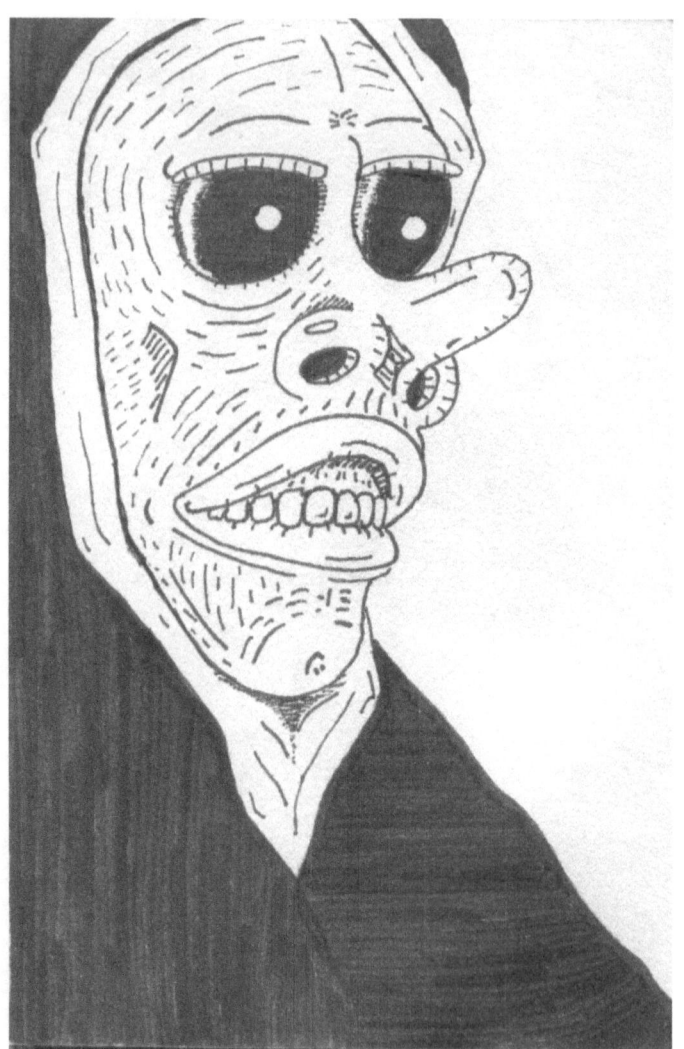

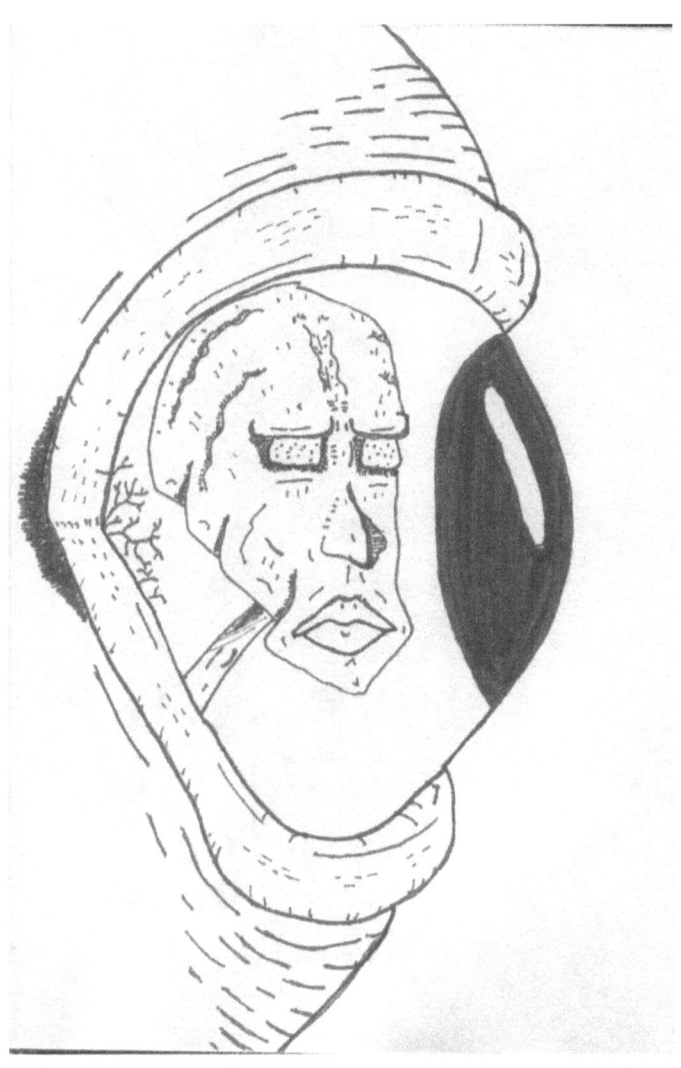

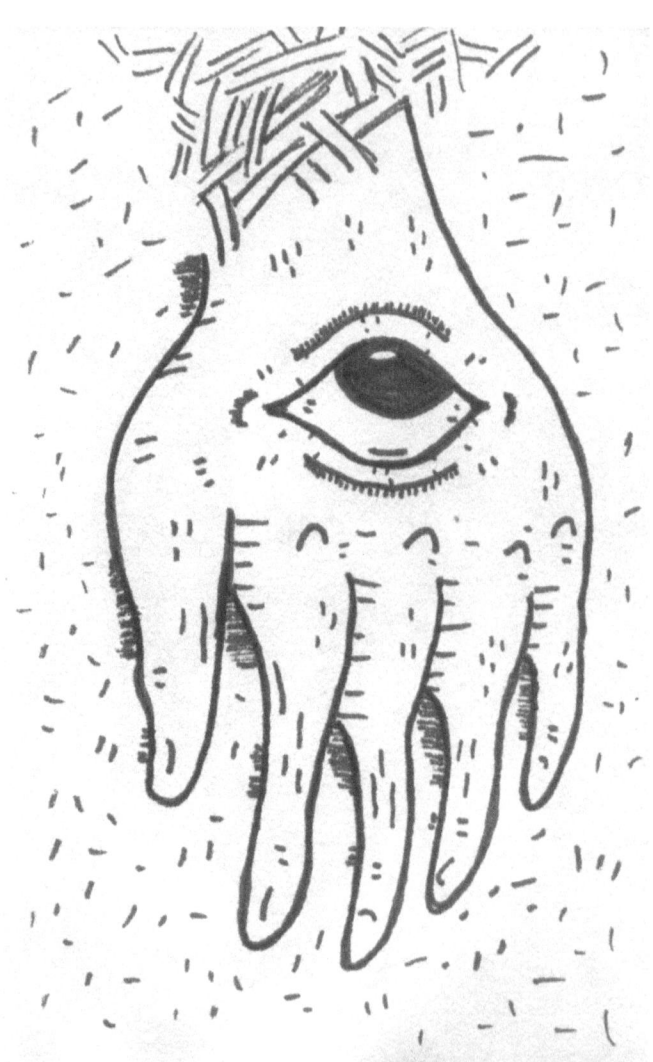

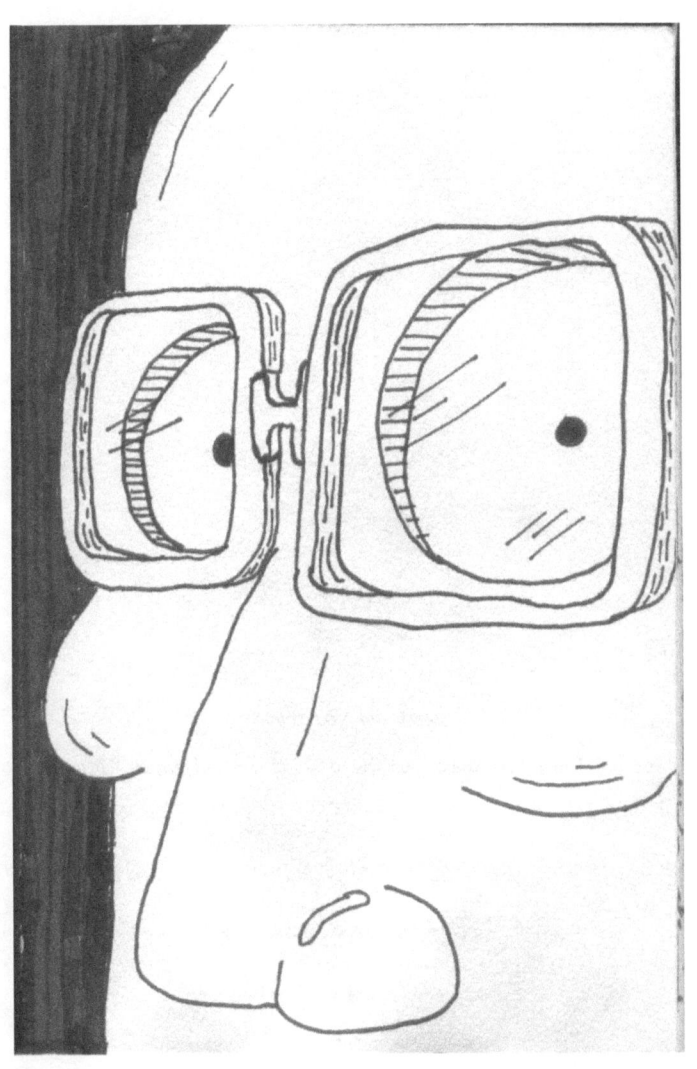

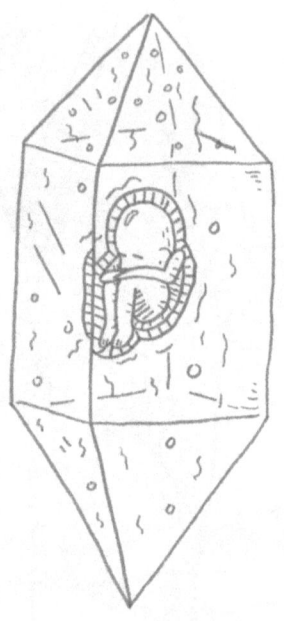

what did you think?

Let me know and check out my ongoing art adventure, I guess.

nstagram: http://instagram.com/thisisvaughnart or @thisisvaughnart

Tumblr: http://thisisvaughnart.tumblr.com/

Email: elkourieworks@gmail.com